DEBUGGING PLAYBOOK

SYSTEM TESTING, ERROR LOCALIZATION, AND VULNERABILITY REMEDIATION

4 BOOKS IN 1

BOOK 1
DEBUGGING PLAYBOOK: SYSTEM TESTING FUNDAMENTALS

BOOK 2
DEBUGGING PLAYBOOK: MASTERING ERROR LOCALIZATION TECHNIQUES

BOOK 3
DEBUGGING PLAYBOOK: ADVANCED STRATEGIES FOR VULNERABILITY REMEDIATION

BOOK 4
DEBUGGING PLAYBOOK: EXPERT APPROACHES TO COMPREHENSIVE SYSTEM TESTING AND SECURITY

ROB BOTWRIGHT

Published by Rob Botwright
Library of Congress Cataloging-in-Publication Data
ISBN 978-1-83938-695-4
Cover design by Rizzo

Disclaimer

The contents of this book are based on extensive research and the best available historical sources. However, the author and publisher make no claims, promises, or guarantees about the accuracy, completeness, or adequacy of the information contained herein. The information in this book is provided on an "as is" basis, and the author and publisher disclaim any and all liability for any errors, omissions, or inaccuracies in the information or for any actions taken in reliance on such information. The opinions and views expressed in this book are those of the author and do not necessarily reflect the official policy or position of any organization or individual mentioned in this book. Any reference to specific people, places, or events is intended only to provide historical context and is not intended to defame or malign any group, individual, or entity. The information in this book is intended for educational and entertainment purposes only. It is not intended to be a substitute for professional advice or judgment. Readers are encouraged to conduct their own research and to seek professional advice where appropriate. Every effort has been made to obtain necessary permissions and acknowledgments for all images and other copyrighted material used in this book. Any errors or omissions in this regard are unintentional, and the author and publisher will correct them in future editions.

BOOK 1 - DEBUGGING PLAYBOOK: SYSTEM TESTING FUNDAMENTALS

BOOK 2 - DEBUGGING PLAYBOOK: MASTERING ERROR LOCALIZATION TECHNIQUES

BOOK 3 - DEBUGGING PLAYBOOK: ADVANCED STRATEGIES FOR VULNERABILITY REMEDIATION

BOOK 4 - DEBUGGING PLAYBOOK: EXPERT APPROACHES TO COMPREHENSIVE SYSTEM TESTING AND SECURITY

Introduction

Welcome to the "Debugging Playbook" bundle, a comprehensive collection of books designed to equip you with the essential knowledge, skills, and strategies needed to navigate the intricate world of software debugging. In today's fast-paced and ever-evolving technological landscape, the ability to effectively debug software systems, localize errors, and remediate vulnerabilities is crucial for ensuring the reliability, security, and performance of software applications.

The "Debugging Playbook" bundle comprises four distinct volumes, each focusing on a critical aspect of debugging:
Book 1: Debugging Playbook: System Testing Fundamentals
Book 2: Debugging Playbook: Mastering Error Localization Techniques Book 3: Debugging Playbook: Advanced Strategies for Vulnerability Remediation Book 4: Debugging Playbook: Expert Approaches to Comprehensive System Testing and Security

In Book 1, you will delve into the fundamentals of system testing, learning essential concepts, methodologies, and best practices for ensuring the quality and reliability of software systems. From understanding the fundamentals of system testing to deploying effective testing frameworks, this book will provide you with a solid foundation in software testing.

Book 2 takes you on a journey into the intricate world of error localization, offering advanced techniques and methodologies for identifying, isolating, and resolving software bugs. Through practical examples, case studies, and hands-on exercises, you will hone your skills in pinpointing and troubleshooting a wide range of software defects.

In Book 3, you will explore advanced strategies for vulnerability remediation, learning how to identify, prioritize, and mitigate security vulnerabilities in software applications. From understanding common security threats to implementing proactive security measures, this book will empower you to strengthen the security posture of your software systems and protect against evolving cyber threats.

Finally, Book 4 introduces expert-level approaches and techniques for comprehensive system testing and security. From incorporating security into the testing process to leveraging advanced debugging tools and methodologies, this book will provide you with the insights and strategies needed to elevate your debugging skills to the next level and ensure the resilience and reliability of your software applications.

Whether you are a seasoned software developer, a QA engineer, or a security professional, the "Debugging Playbook" bundle offers a comprehensive roadmap for mastering the art and science of debugging. Each book is filled with practical insights, real-world examples, and expert advice to help you overcome the challenges of software debugging and deliver more robust, secure, and reliable software solutions. So, dive in, explore the depths of software debugging, and embark on a journey towards becoming a debugging expert.

BOOK 1
DEBUGGING PLAYBOOK
SYSTEM TESTING FUNDAMENTALS

ROB BOTWRIGHT

Chapter 1: Introduction to System Testing

Software testing is a critical component of the software development lifecycle (SDLC). It ensures that the developed software meets the desired quality standards, is free from defects, and functions as expected. Next, we will delve into the fundamentals of software testing, exploring its importance, key concepts, and various testing techniques.

Importance of Software Testing: Software testing plays a pivotal role in ensuring the reliability, functionality, and performance of software applications. By systematically identifying and rectifying defects, testing helps in enhancing the overall quality of the software product. Moreover, thorough testing instills confidence in stakeholders and end-users regarding the reliability of the software.

Types of Software Testing: There are several types of software testing, each serving a distinct purpose in the SDLC. These include:

Unit Testing: Unit testing involves testing individual components or modules of the software in isolation. It is typically performed by developers using frameworks such as JUnit for Java or NUnit for .NET.

Integration Testing: Integration testing verifies the interactions between different modules or components of the software. Techniques like top-down and bottom-up integration testing are commonly employed to ensure seamless integration.

System Testing: System testing evaluates the entire software system to ensure that it meets specified requirements and functions as expected in its intended environment. Test cases cover functional, performance, and security aspects of the system.

Acceptance Testing: Acceptance testing involves validating the software against predefined acceptance criteria to determine whether it meets user expectations. This testing phase is often performed by end-users or stakeholders.

Test Case Development: Test cases serve as the foundation of software testing, outlining the steps to be executed and the expected outcomes. The process of test case development involves:

Requirement Analysis: Understanding the software requirements to derive test scenarios and identify testable features.

Test Scenario Identification: Identifying various scenarios to be tested, covering both positive and negative scenarios.

Test Case Design: Designing detailed test cases, including preconditions, steps to execute, and expected results.

Test Data Preparation: Preparing relevant test data to execute test cases effectively.

Test Execution and Reporting: Once test cases are developed, they are executed to identify defects and verify software functionality. Test execution involves:

Test Environment Setup: Configuring the test environment to mirror the production environment, including hardware, software, and network configurations.

Executing Test Cases: Running test cases as per the defined test plan and documenting the outcomes.

Defect Logging: Recording any deviations from expected results as defects in a defect tracking system like JIRA or Bugzilla.

Test Reporting: Generating comprehensive test reports summarizing test results, defect metrics, and overall test coverage.

Regression Testing Techniques: Regression testing ensures that new changes or enhancements do not adversely impact existing functionality. Common regression testing techniques include:

Re-running Test Cases: Re-executing existing test cases to validate unchanged functionality.

Automated Regression Testing: Automating repetitive test cases using tools like Selenium WebDriver or TestNG.

Selective Regression Testing: Prioritizing test cases based on risk analysis and focusing on critical areas affected by changes.

In summary, software testing is an indispensable aspect of software development, ensuring quality, reliability, and user satisfaction. By understanding the fundamentals of software testing and adopting appropriate testing techniques, software teams can deliver robust and reliable software products to meet user needs and expectations.

System testing is a crucial phase in the software development lifecycle (SDLC) that focuses on evaluating the integrated system to ensure its functionality, reliability, and performance. This chapter explores the significance of system testing, its role in software development, and the benefits it brings to organizations and end-users.

Ensuring Functional Integrity: One of the primary objectives of system testing is to verify that the software system behaves as expected and meets the specified requirements. By systematically testing the entire system, including its interactions with external dependencies, system testing helps identify and rectify functional defects that may arise due to integration issues or incorrect implementation.

Identifying Integration Issues: In complex software applications composed of multiple modules or components, integration issues often arise when individual components interact with each other. System testing allows organizations to detect and address integration problems early in the development lifecycle, ensuring seamless interaction between different system elements.

Validating Performance and Scalability: System testing is instrumental in assessing the performance and scalability of software systems under various conditions. By subjecting the system to simulated workloads, stress tests, and performance benchmarks, organizations can identify performance bottlenecks, resource constraints, and scalability limitations. Performance testing tools like Apache JMeter or LoadRunner enable organizations to conduct load testing, stress testing, and scalability testing efficiently.

Enhancing Software Reliability: Reliability is a critical aspect of software quality, particularly in mission-critical applications where system failures can have severe consequences. System testing helps uncover defects related to reliability, such as memory leaks, race conditions, or unexpected system crashes. By identifying and addressing reliability issues, organizations can improve the stability and robustness of their software systems.

Validating Security Controls: Security vulnerabilities pose a significant risk to software systems, exposing them to potential cyber threats and data breaches. System testing includes security testing activities aimed at identifying vulnerabilities, assessing security controls, and verifying compliance with security standards and regulations. Techniques such as penetration testing, vulnerability scanning, and security code reviews help organizations identify and mitigate security risks effectively.

Mitigating Business Risks: Software failures and defects can have far-reaching consequences for organizations, including financial losses, reputational damage, and legal liabilities. System testing plays a critical role in mitigating business risks by identifying defects early in the development process, reducing the likelihood of costly rework, product recalls, or service disruptions. By ensuring the quality and reliability of software systems, organizations can minimize business risks and safeguard their investments.

Compliance and Regulatory Requirements: In regulated industries such as healthcare, finance, or aviation, compliance with industry standards and regulatory requirements is paramount. System testing helps organizations validate that software systems comply with relevant standards, regulations, and industry best practices. By conducting compliance testing and documenting adherence to regulatory requirements, organizations can demonstrate due diligence and ensure legal compliance.

Improving User Satisfaction: Ultimately, the success of a software system depends on its ability to meet the needs and expectations of end-users. System testing helps validate user requirements, ensure usability, and enhance overall user satisfaction. By delivering software systems that are functional, reliable, and user-friendly, organizations can build trust and loyalty among their user base, leading to increased adoption and customer satisfaction.

In summary, system testing plays a vital role in ensuring the quality, reliability, and security of software systems. By systematically evaluating the integrated system, identifying defects, and mitigating risks, system testing helps organizations deliver high-quality software products that meet user needs and regulatory requirements. Embracing system testing as an integral part of the software development process enables organizations to minimize business risks, enhance user satisfaction, and achieve success in today's competitive market landscape.

Chapter 2: Understanding Test Environments

Test environments play a crucial role in software testing, providing a controlled setup for evaluating the functionality, performance, and reliability of software systems. Next, we explore the various types of test environments used in software development, their characteristics, and their significance in the testing process.

Development Environment: The development environment is where software developers write, compile, and test code before it is integrated into the larger system. It typically consists of development tools, compilers, and libraries required for software development. Developers often use version control systems like Git or Subversion to manage code changes and collaborate with team members.

Command: To clone a Git repository in the development environment, you can use the following CLI command:

bashCopy code

```
git clone <repository_url>
```

Unit Testing Environment: Unit testing environments are dedicated setups for running unit tests, which evaluate individual components or modules of the software in isolation. Unit testing frameworks like JUnit, NUnit, or pytest provide tools for writing and executing unit tests. These environments are lightweight and focused, enabling developers to validate the behavior of specific code units.

Command: To run unit tests using the pytest framework in a Python environment, you can use the following CLI command:

```bash
Copy code
pytest <test_file.py>
```

Integration Testing Environment: Integration testing environments assess the interactions between different modules or components of the software. They ensure that integrated components function as expected and communicate effectively with each other. Integration testing environments may require specialized infrastructure, including databases, APIs, and middleware, to simulate real-world interactions.

Command: To deploy a Docker container for simulating a database in an integration testing environment, you can use the following CLI command:

```bash
Copy code
docker run --name <container_name> -e MYSQL_ROOT_PASSWORD=<password> -d mysql:<version>
```

System Testing Environment: System testing environments evaluate the entire software system to verify its compliance with specified requirements and assess its overall functionality. These environments closely resemble the production environment in terms of hardware, software, and network configurations. System testing environments may utilize virtualization or cloud computing technologies to replicate production environments accurately.

Command: To provision a virtual machine using VMware Workstation for system testing, you can use the following CLI command:

```bash
Copy code
vmrun -T ws create <vmx_file> [gui|nogui]
```

User Acceptance Testing (UAT) Environment: User acceptance testing environments involve end-users or stakeholders validating the software against predefined acceptance criteria. These environments reflect the production environment as closely as possible to ensure accurate assessment by users. UAT environments may require data migration, configuration, and user training to facilitate testing by non-technical users.

Command: To import production data into the UAT environment using a database migration tool like Flyway, you can use the following CLI command:

bashCopy code

```
flyway migrate -url=<jdbc_url> -user=<username> -password=<password>
```

In summary, test environments are essential for conducting effective software testing throughout the development lifecycle. By understanding the types of test environments available and their respective purposes, organizations can establish robust testing processes and infrastructure to ensure the quality, reliability, and performance of their software systems. Whether it's unit testing, integration testing, system testing, or user acceptance testing, selecting the appropriate test environment is critical for achieving successful outcomes in software development projects.

Setting up test environments is a critical step in software testing, ensuring that testers have the necessary infrastructure and resources to conduct comprehensive testing activities. This chapter explores the process of setting up test environments, including the selection of hardware and software components, configuration management, and deployment techniques.

Selection of Hardware and Software Components: The first step in setting up a test environment is to identify the hardware and software components required to support testing activities. This includes selecting suitable hardware platforms, operating systems, databases, and third-party dependencies. The choice of components may vary depending on the nature of the software application, the testing objectives, and the available resources.

Command: To check the hardware specifications of a Linux server using the command line, you can use the following CLI command:

bashCopy code

```
lshw
```

Configuration Management: Configuration management plays a crucial role in maintaining consistency and repeatability across test environments. Configuration management tools such as Ansible, Puppet, or Chef enable organizations to automate the provisioning, configuration, and management of test infrastructure. By defining infrastructure as code (IaC), organizations can easily replicate test environments and ensure consistency across development, testing, and production environments.

Command: To deploy infrastructure using Ansible playbooks, you can use the following CLI command:

bashCopy code

```
ansible-playbook <playbook.yml>
```

Virtualization and Containerization: Virtualization and containerization technologies provide lightweight and scalable solutions for setting up test environments. Virtual machines (VMs) allow testers to create isolated environments with virtualized hardware, while containers offer lightweight, portable environments for running applications and services. Tools like VMware, VirtualBox, Docker, and Kubernetes facilitate the creation and management of virtualized and containerized test environments.

Command: To create a Docker container for a web application, you can use the following CLI command:

bashCopy code

```
docker run -d -p 8080:80 --name <container_name> <image_name>
```

Cloud Computing: Cloud computing platforms offer on-demand access to scalable computing resources, making them ideal for setting up test environments. Public cloud providers like Amazon Web Services (AWS), Microsoft Azure, and Google Cloud Platform (GCP) offer a wide range of services for provisioning virtual machines, storage, networking, and other infrastructure components. Organizations can leverage cloud-based test environments to achieve flexibility, scalability, and cost-effectiveness in their testing activities.

Command: To create a virtual machine instance on AWS EC2 using the AWS CLI, you can use the following CLI command:

bashCopy code

```
aws ec2 run-instances --image-id <ami_id> --instance-type <instance_type> --key-name <key_pair_name> --subnet-id <subnet_id>
```

Test Data Management: Effective test data management is essential for setting up realistic test environments that mimic production scenarios. Test data management tools and techniques enable organizations to generate, manipulate, and maintain test data sets for different testing scenarios. This includes anonymizing sensitive data, generating synthetic data, and managing data dependencies to ensure test data integrity and privacy.

Command: To import test data into a MySQL database using the MySQL command-line client, you can use the following CLI command:

bashCopy code

```
mysql -u <username> -p <database_name> < <sql_file.sql>
```

In summary, setting up test environments requires careful planning, selection of appropriate tools and technologies, and automation of infrastructure provisioning and configuration. By leveraging hardware virtualization, containerization, cloud computing, and configuration management practices, organizations can establish robust and scalable test environments to support their testing activities effectively. Effective test environment setup contributes to the overall success of software testing initiatives, enabling organizations to deliver high-quality software products that meet user needs and expectations.

Chapter 3: Test Case Development

Test cases form the cornerstone of software testing, providing a systematic approach to validate the functionality, performance, and reliability of software systems. Next, we delve into the art and science of writing effective test cases, exploring best practices, techniques, and tools to create comprehensive and actionable test cases.

Understanding Test Case Structure: Before delving into the specifics of writing test cases, it's essential to understand the structure of a typical test case. A well-structured test case typically consists of the following elements:

Test Case ID: A unique identifier for the test case, often in the form of a numerical or alphanumeric code.

Test Case Title: A descriptive title that succinctly summarizes the objective or scenario being tested.

Test Case Description: A detailed description of the test scenario, including preconditions, inputs, expected outcomes, and any specific steps to be executed.

Test Steps: Sequential steps to be followed to execute the test case, including actions to be performed and expected results at each step.

Expected Results: Clear and unambiguous expectations of the outcomes or behaviors expected when executing the test case.

Actual Results: Optionally, a field to record the actual outcomes observed during test execution, to facilitate result comparison and defect reporting.

Command: To create a new test case document using a text editor like Vim, you can use the following CLI command:

bashCopy code

```
vim test_case_<id>.txt
```

Identifying Test Scenarios: Effective test case writing begins with identifying relevant test scenarios that cover various aspects of the software functionality. Test scenarios are specific instances or conditions under which the software is tested to validate its behavior. Testers can derive test scenarios from requirements documents, user stories, use cases, and other sources of project documentation.

Technique: One effective technique for identifying test scenarios is boundary value analysis, which involves testing the boundaries between valid and invalid input values. For example, if a text field accepts input between 1 and 100 characters, test scenarios would include inputs at the lower and upper boundaries, as well as just inside and outside these boundaries.

Writing Clear and Concise Test Steps: Each test case should include clear and concise test steps that guide testers through the execution of the test scenario. Test steps should be written in a sequential manner, using simple language and avoiding ambiguity. Each step should represent a specific action or interaction with the software under test, along with the expected outcome.

Example: Test Case Title: Login Functionality Verification Test Case Description: Verify that users can successfully log in to the application using valid credentials. Test Steps: Navigate to the login page.

Enter valid username and password.

Click on the login button. Expected Results: The user should be redirected to the home page after successful login.

Ensuring Test Coverage: A key aspect of effective test case writing is ensuring comprehensive test coverage, which involves testing all relevant functionalities, features, and use cases of the software. Testers should strive to cover both positive and negative scenarios, boundary cases, error handling, and integration points to uncover potential defects and ensure robust software quality.

Tool: Test case management tools like TestRail, Zephyr, or QTest enable testers to organize, prioritize, and track test cases, ensuring comprehensive test coverage across various testing cycles and releases. These tools also facilitate collaboration among team members and provide visibility into test execution progress and results.

Command: To create a new test case in TestRail using the web interface, you can follow these steps:

Log in to TestRail.

Navigate to the Test Cases tab.

Click on the Add Test Case button.

Enter the test case details, including title, description, steps, and expected results.

Click Save to add the test case to the test case repository.

In summary, writing effective test cases is a critical aspect of software testing, enabling testers to systematically validate the functionality, performance, and reliability of software systems. By understanding the structure of a test case, identifying relevant test scenarios, writing clear and concise test steps, ensuring comprehensive test coverage, and leveraging test case management tools, organizations can create robust and actionable test cases that drive quality and ensure successful software delivery. Effective test case writing is not only a skill but also an art, honed through experience, collaboration, and continuous improvement, contributing to the overall success of software testing initiatives.

Test case management is a critical aspect of software testing, providing a structured approach to creating, organizing, executing, and tracking test cases throughout the testing lifecycle. Next, we explore the importance of test case management, key components of a test case management system, best practices, and tools to streamline the test case management process.

Importance of Test Case Management: Effective test case management is essential for ensuring comprehensive test coverage, tracking test execution progress, identifying defects, and facilitating collaboration among team members. A robust test case management process enables organizations to maintain traceability between requirements, test cases, and defects, ensuring that software meets user expectations and quality standards.

Components of Test Case Management: A test case management system typically consists of the following components:

Test Case Repository: A centralized repository for storing test cases, including details such as test case title, description, steps, expected results, priority, and status.

Test Planning: The process of defining test objectives, scope, resources, and timelines for testing activities. Test planning involves identifying test scenarios, estimating effort, and prioritizing test cases based on risk and impact.

Test Execution: The process of running test cases and recording test results. Test execution involves assigning test cases to testers, executing them in the test environment, and documenting outcomes.

Defect Management: The process of identifying, reporting, tracking, and resolving defects discovered during testing. Defect management includes capturing defect details, assigning severity and priority, and verifying defect fixes.

Reporting and Analysis: The process of generating test reports, metrics, and dashboards to provide insights into test coverage, execution progress, defect trends, and overall testing effectiveness.

Techniques for Test Case Management: Several techniques can be employed to streamline test case management and enhance testing efficiency:

Test Case Organization: Organizing test cases into logical categories or folders based on modules, features, or functional areas helps maintain clarity and facilitates easy navigation and retrieval.

Version Control: Using version control systems like Git or Subversion to manage test case artifacts ensures traceability, facilitates collaboration, and enables rollback to previous versions if needed.

Test Case Prioritization: Prioritizing test cases based on risk, business impact, and criticality helps focus testing efforts on high-priority areas and ensures maximum coverage within available resources.

Test Case Traceability: Establishing traceability links between requirements, test cases, and defects helps ensure alignment between testing activities and project objectives, enabling stakeholders to track progress and make informed decisions.

Automation: Automating repetitive testing tasks, such as test case execution, data setup, and result verification, using tools like Selenium, Appium, or JUnit, helps improve testing efficiency, reduce manual effort, and accelerate release cycles.

Test Case Management Tools: Numerous test case management tools are available to streamline test case management processes and enhance collaboration among testing teams. Some popular test case management tools include:

TestRail: TestRail is a comprehensive test case management tool that provides features for test case creation, execution, reporting, and defect management. It offers integration with various issue tracking systems and test automation tools.

Zephyr: Zephyr is a robust test management solution designed for Agile and DevOps teams. It offers features for test case creation, execution, and reporting, along with real-time visibility into testing progress.

qTest: qTest is a cloud-based test management platform that enables teams to manage test cases, execute tests, track defects, and generate test reports. It offers integrations with popular CI/CD tools and test automation frameworks.

Command: To create a new test case in TestRail using the command-line interface (CLI), you can use the following command:

bashCopy code

```
testrail add_test_case --title "Test Case Title" --section-id <section_id> --type <test_type> --priority <priority>
```

In summary, effective test case management is essential for ensuring the success of software testing initiatives and delivering high-quality software products. By implementing robust test case management processes, leveraging appropriate techniques, and utilizing test case management tools, organizations can streamline testing activities, enhance collaboration among team members, and achieve greater efficiency and effectiveness in their testing efforts. Test case management is not just a procedural task but a strategic endeavor that requires careful planning, execution, and continuous improvement to meet evolving business needs and quality standards.

Chapter 4: Test Execution and Reporting

Test execution is a crucial phase in the software testing lifecycle, where test cases are executed, and actual results are compared against expected outcomes to validate the behavior of the software under test. Next, we delve into the test execution process, covering its importance, key steps, best practices, and tools to facilitate efficient test execution.

Importance of Test Execution: Test execution is the stage where the rubber meets the road in software testing, allowing testers to validate the functionality, performance, and reliability of the software system. It is the final step in the testing process before software is released to production, making it a critical determinant of software quality and user satisfaction. Effective test execution helps identify defects early, minimize business risks, and ensure that software meets user requirements and expectations.

Key Steps in Test Execution: The test execution process typically consists of the following key steps:

Test Environment Setup: Configuring the test environment to replicate the production environment, including hardware, software, and network configurations. Test environment setup ensures that test cases are executed under realistic conditions, facilitating accurate validation of software behavior.

Command: To deploy a test environment using infrastructure-as-code (IaC) tools like Terraform, you can use the following CLI command:

bashCopy code

terraform apply

Test Case Selection: Selecting test cases to be executed based on test plans, priorities, and objectives. Test case selection involves identifying high-priority test scenarios, critical functionalities, and regression test cases to ensure comprehensive test coverage within available resources.

Test Execution: Running selected test cases in the test environment and recording actual results. Test execution involves following test steps, inputting test data, interacting with the software under test, and verifying outcomes against expected results.

Defect Reporting: Reporting any deviations from expected results as defects in a defect tracking system. Defect reporting includes capturing defect details, such as description, severity, priority, steps to reproduce, and associated test cases, to facilitate defect resolution by development teams.

Regression Testing: Re-executing regression test cases to ensure that recent changes or enhancements do not introduce new defects or regressions. Regression testing helps maintain software integrity and stability by verifying that existing functionalities remain unaffected by changes.

Best Practices for Test Execution: To ensure effective test execution, testers should adhere to the following best practices:

Thorough Test Planning: Invest time in comprehensive test planning to define clear test objectives, scope, and success criteria. A well-defined test plan serves as a roadmap for test execution and helps prioritize testing activities based on business priorities and risks.

Test Case Documentation: Document test cases accurately, including test steps, expected results, preconditions, and postconditions. Clear and concise test case documentation ensures that testers understand test scenarios and execute them consistently.

Environment Validation: Validate the test environment before test execution to ensure that it is stable, reliable, and properly configured. Environment validation includes verifying hardware, software, network connectivity, and access permissions to prevent test execution issues.

Test Data Management: Manage test data effectively to ensure that test cases have access to relevant and valid data sets. Test data management involves creating, anonymizing, and maintaining test data repositories to support various testing scenarios and data-driven tests.

Continuous Communication: Maintain open communication channels with stakeholders, development teams, and other relevant parties throughout the test execution process. Regular status updates, defect triage meetings, and progress reports help ensure alignment and facilitate timely issue resolution.

Test Execution Tools: Several test execution tools are available to streamline and automate test execution processes, including:

Test Automation Frameworks: Test automation frameworks like Selenium WebDriver, Appium, and TestNG enable testers to automate the execution of repetitive test cases, regression tests, and end-to-end scenarios across web, mobile, and desktop applications.

Test Management Tools: Test management tools like TestRail, HP ALM, and PractiTest provide features for test case management, test execution, defect tracking, and reporting. These tools offer centralized repositories for test artifacts, real-time visibility into test progress, and collaboration capabilities for testing teams.

Continuous Integration (CI) Tools: CI tools like Jenkins, Travis CI, and CircleCI integrate test execution into the software development pipeline, automating the execution of tests whenever code changes are made. CI/CD pipelines enable organizations to achieve faster feedback loops, accelerate release cycles, and maintain software quality.

 In summary, test execution is a critical phase in the software testing lifecycle, where test cases are executed to validate the behavior of the software under test. By following best practices, leveraging appropriate tools, and ensuring effective communication and collaboration, organizations can streamline test execution processes, identify defects early, and deliver high-quality software products that meet user needs and expectations. Test execution is not just a task but a strategic endeavor that requires careful planning, execution, and continuous improvement to achieve successful testing outcomes and ensure software quality.

Test reporting and analysis play a pivotal role in software testing, providing stakeholders with valuable insights into the quality, progress, and effectiveness of testing activities. Next, we explore the significance of test reporting and analysis, key components of test reports, best practices for generating meaningful reports, and techniques for analyzing test data to drive informed decision-making.

Components of Test Reports: A well-structured test report typically includes the following components:

Executive Summary: A concise overview of test results, highlighting key findings, achievements, and areas of concern. The executive summary provides stakeholders with a high-level understanding of the testing status and outcomes.

Test Coverage Metrics: Metrics indicating the extent to which testing activities have covered various aspects of the software, including requirements coverage, code coverage, and test case coverage. Test coverage metrics help assess the thoroughness and effectiveness of testing efforts.

Defect Metrics: Metrics related to defects discovered during testing, including defect density, defect severity distribution, defect aging, and defect closure rates. Defect metrics provide insights into the quality of the software under test and help prioritize defect resolution efforts.

Test Execution Metrics: Metrics related to test execution activities, such as test case execution status, test pass/fail rates, test execution trends over time, and test execution duration. Test execution metrics help assess testing progress, identify bottlenecks, and track testing efficiency.

Regression Test Results: Results of regression testing activities, indicating whether recent changes or enhancements have introduced new defects or regressions. Regression test results help assess the impact of changes on existing functionalities and ensure software stability.

Best Practices for Test Reporting: To generate meaningful and effective test reports, testers should adhere to the following best practices:

Tailor Reports to Audience: Customize test reports to suit the needs and interests of different stakeholders, such as project managers, development teams, and executive leadership. Tailoring reports to the audience ensures that relevant information is presented in a clear and actionable manner.

Use Visualizations: Incorporate charts, graphs, and other visualizations to present test data in a visually appealing and easily understandable format. Visualizations help stakeholders quickly grasp trends, patterns, and anomalies in test data.

Provide Context: Provide context and interpretation for test metrics and results to help stakeholders understand their significance and implications. Contextual information enables stakeholders to make informed decisions based on test data.

Focus on Key Metrics: Prioritize key metrics and findings in test reports to avoid information overload and ensure that the most critical insights are highlighted. Focusing on key metrics helps keep test reports concise and actionable.

Include Recommendations: Offer recommendations for improvement based on test findings and analysis. Providing actionable recommendations helps stakeholders address identified issues and enhance the overall quality of the software.

Techniques for Test Data Analysis: Several techniques can be employed to analyze test data and derive actionable insights:

Trend Analysis: Analyze test metrics over time to identify trends, patterns, and anomalies in testing activities. Trend analysis helps stakeholders understand testing progress, predict future outcomes, and identify areas for improvement.

Root Cause Analysis: Investigate the root causes of defects and testing issues to address underlying problems and prevent recurrence. Root cause analysis involves identifying contributing factors, analyzing dependencies, and implementing corrective actions.

Comparative Analysis: Compare test results across different releases, builds, or environments to assess improvement or degradation in software quality. Comparative analysis helps identify trends, evaluate the impact of changes, and benchmark performance against established targets.

Risk-based Analysis: Prioritize testing efforts based on risk factors such as business impact, likelihood of occurrence, and severity of consequences. Risk-based analysis helps focus testing resources on high-risk areas and optimize testing coverage.

Cross-functional Analysis: Collaborate with other teams, such as development, operations, and business stakeholders, to analyze test data from multiple perspectives and gain holistic insights into software quality. Cross-functional analysis promotes collaboration, alignment, and shared accountability for quality.

Tools for Test Reporting and Analysis: Several tools and frameworks can facilitate test reporting and analysis, including:

Test Management Tools: Test management tools like TestRail, HP ALM, and Jira provide features for generating test reports, tracking test execution, and analyzing test data. These tools offer customizable dashboards, reporting templates, and integrations with other testing tools.

Business Intelligence (BI) Tools: BI tools like Tableau, Power BI, and QlikView enable advanced data visualization, reporting, and analysis capabilities. BI tools can be used to create interactive dashboards, drill-down reports, and ad-hoc analyses based on test data.

Statistical Analysis Tools: Statistical analysis tools like R, Python with pandas, and MATLAB provide capabilities for performing advanced statistical analyses on test data. These tools can be used to calculate descriptive statistics, conduct hypothesis testing, and model relationships between variables.

In summary, test reporting and analysis are essential components of the software testing process, providing stakeholders with valuable insights into testing activities, outcomes, and quality. By following best practices, leveraging appropriate techniques, and utilizing relevant tools, organizations can generate meaningful test reports, analyze test data effectively, and make informed decisions to improve software quality and achieve project objectives. Test reporting and analysis are not just administrative tasks but strategic activities that contribute to the success of software testing initiatives and ultimately, the delivery of high-quality software products.

Chapter 5: Regression Testing Techniques

Regression testing is a fundamental aspect of software testing that ensures existing functionalities remain unaffected by code changes, bug fixes, or system enhancements. Next, we delve into the concept of regression testing, its importance in software development, key principles, techniques, and best practices for effective regression testing.

Importance of Regression Testing: As software evolves through multiple iterations and releases, developers frequently introduce changes to fix defects, enhance features, or optimize performance. However, these changes have the potential to introduce new defects or regressions, inadvertently impacting existing functionalities. Regression testing mitigates this risk by systematically retesting modified or affected areas of the software to ensure that no unintended side effects occur.

Key Principles of Regression Testing: Regression testing is guided by several key principles, including:

Comprehensive Coverage: Regression testing aims to cover critical functionalities, integrations, and interactions within the software system to identify potential regressions across different modules and components.

Selective Test Case Selection: Not all test cases need to be executed during regression testing. Test cases are selectively chosen based on factors such as risk, impact, and likelihood of regression, to optimize testing efforts and minimize test execution time.

Prioritization: Regression test cases are prioritized based on factors such as business criticality, frequency of use, and likelihood of regression. High-priority test cases are executed first to address critical functionalities and minimize business risks.

Automation: Automation plays a crucial role in regression testing by enabling the rapid execution of repetitive test cases across multiple iterations. Automated regression tests help streamline testing efforts, accelerate feedback loops, and ensure consistency in test execution.

Techniques for Regression Testing: Several techniques can be employed to perform regression testing effectively:

Retest All: In this technique, all existing test cases are re-executed to ensure that no regressions have occurred. While this approach provides comprehensive coverage, it can be time-consuming and impractical for large test suites.

Regression Test Selection: This technique involves selecting a subset of test cases from the existing test suite based on the impact of changes or areas affected by recent modifications. Regression test selection techniques include code coverage analysis, impact analysis, and risk-based prioritization.

Test Case Prioritization: Test cases are prioritized based on factors such as criticality, frequency of use, and likelihood of regression. High-priority test cases are executed first to identify critical regressions early in the testing process.

Regression Test Automation: Automation of regression tests using tools like Selenium, TestNG, or JUnit helps streamline test execution, improve testing efficiency, and ensure consistent test coverage across iterations. Automated regression tests are particularly useful for repetitive test scenarios and frequent code changes.

Best Practices for Regression Testing: To ensure effective regression testing, testers should adhere to the following best practices:

Establish Regression Test Suites: Develop and maintain regression test suites containing a comprehensive set of test cases covering critical functionalities, integration points, and common user scenarios. Regression test suites serve as a baseline for regression testing and ensure consistent test coverage across iterations.

Automate Regression Tests: Automate repetitive regression tests using appropriate test automation frameworks and tools to accelerate test execution, minimize manual effort, and ensure consistency in test execution.

Regular Regression Cycles: Schedule regular regression testing cycles at key milestones throughout the software development lifecycle, such as after each sprint, release, or major code change. Regular regression cycles help detect regressions early and prevent them from cascading into larger issues.

Regression Test Environment: Maintain a stable and consistent test environment that closely mirrors the production environment to ensure accurate and reliable regression testing results. Test environments should include relevant hardware, software, configurations, and data sets to simulate real-world usage scenarios.

Regression Testing Tools: Several tools and frameworks can facilitate regression testing, including:

Selenium WebDriver: Selenium WebDriver is a popular open-source automation tool for web application testing. It supports various programming languages and browsers, allowing testers to automate web-based regression tests efficiently.

TestNG: TestNG is a testing framework for Java that supports regression testing, parameterized testing, and data-driven testing. It provides features such as test case grouping, parallel execution, and reporting to streamline regression testing activities.

JUnit: JUnit is a unit testing framework for Java that can also be used for regression testing. It provides annotations, assertions, and test runners to automate and organize regression test cases effectively.

Apache JMeter: Apache JMeter is a performance testing tool that can be used for regression testing of web applications, APIs, and databases. It supports load testing, stress testing, and functional testing, making it suitable for comprehensive regression testing.

In summary, regression testing is a critical aspect of software testing that ensures existing functionalities remain intact and unaffected by changes or enhancements. By following key principles, employing appropriate techniques, and leveraging regression testing best practices and tools, organizations can mitigate the risk of regressions, maintain software quality, and deliver reliable software products to end users. Regression testing is not just a reactive measure but a proactive approach to safeguarding software integrity and ensuring continuous improvement in software development processes.

Regression test selection is a critical aspect of regression testing aimed at optimizing testing efforts by selectively executing a subset of test cases from the existing test suite. Next, we explore various regression test selection techniques, their importance in software testing, implementation strategies, and best practices for effective regression test selection.

Importance of Regression Test Selection: As software systems grow in complexity and size, the size of the test suite also increases, leading to longer test execution times and higher testing costs. Regression test selection mitigates these challenges by identifying and executing only those test cases that are affected by recent changes or modifications, thereby reducing test execution time, optimizing resource utilization, and accelerating the feedback loop in the software development process.

Key Regression Test Selection Techniques: Several regression test selection techniques can be employed to identify relevant test cases for execution:

Code Coverage Analysis: Code coverage analysis involves determining which portions of the codebase have been modified or impacted by recent changes. Test cases covering these modified code segments are selected for regression testing to ensure that changes do not introduce new defects or regressions.

Command: To generate code coverage reports using a tool like JaCoCo in a Java project, you can use the following Maven command:

bashCopy code

```
mvn clean test jacoco:report
```

Impact Analysis: Impact analysis assesses the impact of recent changes on the overall system by analyzing dependencies, interfaces, and interactions between modules or components. Test cases covering impacted areas are selected for regression testing to verify that changes have not caused unintended side effects.

Change-Based Selection: Change-based selection focuses on identifying test cases related to specific changesets or commits in the version control system. Test cases associated with recent code changes are selected for regression testing to validate the correctness and integrity of the modified code.

Risk-Based Prioritization: Risk-based prioritization prioritizes test cases based on factors such as business criticality, frequency of use, and likelihood of regression. High-risk areas are given priority in regression testing to ensure that critical functionalities remain intact and unaffected by changes.

Implementation Strategies for Regression Test Selection: Implementing regression test selection techniques effectively requires careful planning and execution. Some strategies for successful implementation include:

Automated Tool Support: Leverage automated testing tools and frameworks that support regression test selection techniques, such as code coverage tools, impact analysis tools, and version control integrations. Automated tools streamline the process of identifying relevant test cases for regression testing and ensure consistency and accuracy in test selection.

Integration with CI/CD Pipelines: Integrate regression test selection techniques into the continuous integration and continuous delivery (CI/CD) pipeline to automate the selection and execution of regression tests as part of the software build and deployment process. CI/CD pipelines help maintain a rapid and iterative development cycle while ensuring the integrity and quality of software releases.

Best Practices for Regression Test Selection: To ensure effective regression test selection, testers should follow these best practices:

Regular Test Maintenance: Regularly review and update the regression test suite to reflect changes in the software system, such as new features, bug fixes, or code refactoring. Keeping the regression test suite up-to-date ensures that relevant test cases are selected for regression testing and that obsolete or redundant test cases are removed.

Collaboration with Development Teams: Collaborate closely with development teams to understand upcoming changes, feature enhancements, and bug fixes. Early involvement in the development process helps identify impacted areas and select appropriate test cases for regression testing.

Continuous Monitoring of Test Coverage: Continuously monitor test coverage metrics, such as code coverage and requirements coverage, to assess the effectiveness of regression test selection techniques. Test coverage metrics provide insights into the thoroughness and completeness of regression testing efforts and help identify areas for improvement.

In summary, regression test selection techniques play a crucial role in optimizing testing efforts and ensuring the effectiveness of regression testing in software development projects. By employing appropriate techniques, implementing effective strategies, and following best practices, organizations can streamline regression testing processes, reduce test execution time, and maintain software quality and integrity across multiple iterations and releases. Regression test selection is not just a technical task but a strategic approach to maximizing testing efficiency and achieving faster time-to-market without compromising software reliability and stability.

Chapter 6: Performance Testing Essentials

Performance testing is a crucial aspect of software testing aimed at evaluating the responsiveness, scalability, and stability of a software application under various workload conditions. Next, we explore the fundamentals of performance testing, its importance in software development, key performance metrics, testing types, and best practices for conducting effective performance tests.

Importance of Performance Testing: In today's digital landscape, user expectations for fast and reliable software experiences are higher than ever. Performance testing helps organizations ensure that their software applications meet these expectations by identifying performance bottlenecks, scalability issues, and areas for optimization before the application is deployed to production. By proactively addressing performance issues, organizations can enhance user satisfaction, minimize business risks, and maintain a competitive edge in the market.

Key Performance Metrics: Performance testing evaluates various performance metrics to assess the behavior and characteristics of the software application under test. Some key performance metrics include:

Response Time: The time taken for the system to respond to user actions or requests, such as loading a web page, processing a transaction, or executing a query. Response time is a critical indicator of system responsiveness and user experience.

Throughput: The rate at which the system can process and handle incoming requests or transactions within a specified time frame. Throughput measures the system's capacity to handle concurrent user interactions and is essential for assessing system scalability and capacity planning.

Concurrency: The ability of the system to handle multiple concurrent users or transactions simultaneously without degradation in performance. Concurrency testing evaluates how well the system performs under peak load conditions and helps identify bottlenecks related to resource contention or locking.

Resource Utilization: The utilization of system resources, such as CPU, memory, disk I/O, and network bandwidth, during normal and peak load conditions. Monitoring resource utilization helps identify resource-intensive operations and optimize resource allocation for improved performance.

Types of Performance Testing: Performance testing encompasses several testing types, each focusing on different aspects of system performance:

Load Testing: Load testing evaluates the system's behavior under expected load conditions to determine its capacity, scalability, and response times. Load testing simulates typical user activity levels and assesses how the system performs under various load levels.

Stress Testing: Stress testing assesses the system's resilience and stability under extreme load conditions beyond its normal operating capacity. Stress testing aims to identify performance bottlenecks, failure points, and system limitations under high-stress scenarios.

Soak Testing: Soak testing, also known as endurance testing, evaluates the system's performance and stability over an extended period under sustained load conditions.

Soak testing helps identify memory leaks, resource leaks, and degradation in system performance over time.

Scalability Testing: Scalability testing assesses the system's ability to scale horizontally or vertically to accommodate increasing user loads or data volumes. Scalability testing helps determine the maximum capacity of the system and identifies scalability bottlenecks or constraints.

Best Practices for Performance Testing: To conduct effective performance tests, testers should follow these best practices:

Define Clear Performance Objectives: Clearly define performance objectives, success criteria, and performance acceptance criteria based on business requirements and user expectations. Establishing clear performance goals helps align testing efforts with project objectives and ensures meaningful test results.

Select Representative Workloads: Use realistic and representative workloads that simulate actual user behavior, transaction volumes, and system interactions. Representative workloads help ensure that performance tests accurately reflect real-world usage scenarios and provide actionable insights into system performance.

Monitor and Measure Performance Metrics: Monitor and measure key performance metrics, such as response time, throughput, and resource utilization, during performance tests. Use performance monitoring tools and dashboards to visualize performance metrics in real-time and identify performance bottlenecks.

Isolate Performance Testing Environments: Isolate performance testing environments from production and other testing environments to minimize interference and ensure accurate test results. Dedicated performance testing environments help create controlled testing conditions and prevent resource contention or interference from other activities.

In summary, performance testing is a critical aspect of software testing that evaluates the responsiveness, scalability, and stability of software applications under various workload conditions. By understanding the fundamentals of performance testing, key performance metrics, testing types, and best practices, organizations can conduct effective performance tests to identify and address performance bottlenecks, optimize system performance, and deliver high-quality software products that meet user expectations. Performance testing is not just a technical exercise but a strategic endeavor that contributes to the overall success and competitiveness of software applications in today's fast-paced and demanding digital landscape.

Performance metrics and analysis are essential components of performance testing aimed at evaluating the behavior, efficiency, and effectiveness of software applications under various workload conditions. Next, we delve into the fundamentals of performance metrics, their significance in performance testing, techniques for performance data analysis, and best practices for interpreting and leveraging performance metrics to optimize system performance.

Importance of Performance Metrics: Performance metrics provide quantitative measurements of system behavior, resource utilization, and user experience during performance testing. These metrics serve as indicators of system health, identify performance bottlenecks, and guide optimization efforts to enhance system performance, scalability, and reliability. By analyzing performance metrics, organizations can gain insights into system behavior, identify areas for improvement, and make data-driven decisions to optimize software applications for better user experience and efficiency.

Key Performance Metrics: Performance testing evaluates various performance metrics to assess system behavior and characteristics. Some key performance metrics include:

Response Time: The time taken for the system to respond to user requests or actions, such as loading a web page, processing a transaction, or executing a query. Response time is a critical indicator of system responsiveness and directly impacts user experience.

Throughput: The rate at which the system can process and handle incoming requests or transactions within a specified time frame. Throughput measures the system's capacity to handle concurrent user interactions and is essential for assessing system scalability and performance under load.

Error Rate: The frequency of errors or failures encountered during performance testing, such as timeouts, connection errors, or resource exhaustion. Error rate indicates system stability, reliability, and robustness under varying workload conditions.

Resource Utilization: The utilization of system resources, such as CPU, memory, disk I/O, and network bandwidth, during performance testing. Monitoring resource utilization helps identify resource-intensive operations, optimize resource allocation, and prevent resource contention or saturation.

Techniques for Performance Data Analysis: Several techniques can be employed to analyze performance data effectively:

Statistical Analysis: Statistical analysis involves analyzing performance data using statistical methods and techniques, such as mean, median, standard deviation, and percentiles. Statistical analysis helps identify trends, patterns, and outliers in performance metrics and provides insights into system behavior and performance variability.

Trend Analysis: Trend analysis examines performance metrics over time to identify performance trends, patterns, and deviations from expected behavior. Trend analysis helps assess performance stability, detect performance degradation or improvement, and predict future performance trends.

Correlation Analysis: Correlation analysis examines relationships between different performance metrics to identify dependencies, correlations, and cause-effect relationships. Correlation analysis helps pinpoint performance bottlenecks, root causes of performance issues, and areas for optimization.

Benchmarking: Benchmarking compares performance metrics against predefined benchmarks, industry standards, or performance targets to assess system performance relative to peers or best practices. Benchmarking helps organizations identify performance gaps, set performance goals, and benchmark performance improvements over time.

Best Practices for Performance Metrics and Analysis: To leverage performance metrics effectively, organizations should follow these best practices:

Define Relevant Metrics: Define relevant performance metrics based on project objectives, user requirements, and system characteristics. Select performance metrics that align with performance goals, user expectations, and business objectives to ensure meaningful and actionable performance data.

Establish Baselines: Establish performance baselines by collecting baseline performance data under normal operating conditions. Baselines serve as a reference point for comparison, enabling organizations to identify deviations from expected behavior, detect performance anomalies, and measure performance improvements over time.

Monitor Continuously: Continuously monitor performance metrics during performance testing to track system behavior, detect performance issues in real-time, and identify opportunities for optimization. Use performance monitoring tools and dashboards to visualize performance metrics, set performance thresholds, and trigger alerts for abnormal behavior.

Collaborate Across Teams: Collaborate across development, testing, operations, and business teams to interpret performance metrics, prioritize performance optimization efforts, and implement performance improvements. Cross-functional collaboration helps align performance testing objectives with business goals and ensures a holistic approach to performance optimization.

In summary, performance metrics and analysis are essential components of performance testing aimed at evaluating system behavior, efficiency, and effectiveness under various workload conditions. By understanding the fundamentals of performance metrics, techniques for performance data analysis, and best practices for leveraging performance metrics effectively, organizations can gain insights into system performance, identify areas for improvement, and optimize software applications for better user experience, scalability, and reliability. Performance metrics and analysis are not just technical exercises but strategic endeavors that contribute to the overall success and competitiveness of software applications in today's fast-paced and demanding digital landscape.

Chapter 7: Load and Stress Testing Strategies

Load testing is a fundamental aspect of performance testing that evaluates the behavior and performance of a software application under expected and peak load conditions. Next, we explore the basics of load testing, its significance in software development, key concepts, techniques, and best practices for conducting effective load tests.

Importance of Load Testing: Load testing helps organizations assess how their software applications perform under normal and peak load conditions, ensuring that they can handle the expected user traffic without degradation in performance or downtime. By simulating realistic user loads, load testing identifies performance bottlenecks, scalability issues, and areas for optimization, enabling organizations to deliver reliable, scalable, and high-performing software applications to end-users.

Key Concepts of Load Testing: Load testing involves several key concepts and components:

Load Generation: Load generators simulate virtual users or client requests to generate the desired load on the system under test. Load generation tools generate concurrent user activity, HTTP requests, database queries, or API calls to simulate real-world usage scenarios.

Virtual Users: Virtual users represent simulated users or clients interacting with the software application during load testing. Virtual users perform actions such as browsing web pages, submitting forms, or executing transactions to generate load on the system.

Scenarios: Load testing scenarios define the sequence of user actions, transactions, or requests simulated by virtual users during load testing. Scenarios specify the flow of user interactions, think times, pacing, and data variations to simulate realistic usage patterns.

Metrics: Load testing metrics measure various aspects of system performance, such as response time, throughput, error rate, and resource utilization. Load testing metrics provide insights into system behavior, identify performance bottlenecks, and guide optimization efforts.

Techniques for Load Testing: Several techniques can be employed to conduct effective load testing:

Stress Testing: Stress testing evaluates the system's behavior under extreme load conditions beyond its normal operating capacity. Stress testing helps identify performance bottlenecks, failure points, and system limitations under high-stress scenarios.

Soak Testing: Soak testing, also known as endurance testing, assesses the system's performance and stability over an extended period under sustained load conditions. Soak testing helps identify memory leaks, resource leaks, and degradation in system performance over time.

Volume Testing: Volume testing evaluates the system's behavior when subjected to large volumes of data or transactions. Volume testing assesses the system's scalability, data handling capabilities, and performance under increasing data loads.

Peak Load Testing: Peak load testing evaluates the system's performance under peak load conditions, such as during seasonal peaks, promotional events, or periods of high user activity. Peak load testing helps ensure that the system can handle peak loads without degradation in performance or downtime.

Best Practices for Load Testing: To conduct effective load tests, organizations should follow these best practices:

Define Realistic Scenarios: Define load testing scenarios that simulate realistic usage patterns, user behaviors, and workload variations. Realistic scenarios help ensure that load tests accurately reflect real-world usage scenarios and provide meaningful insights into system performance.

Gradual Ramp-up: Gradually ramp up the load during load testing to simulate a gradual increase in user activity and identify performance thresholds, scalability limits, and system breaking points. Gradual ramp-up helps prevent sudden spikes in load that may overwhelm the system and distort test results.

Monitor Performance Metrics: Continuously monitor performance metrics, such as response time, throughput, error rate, and resource utilization, during load testing. Performance monitoring helps detect performance bottlenecks, identify areas for optimization, and ensure that performance goals are met.

Iterative Testing: Conduct iterative load testing cycles to validate performance improvements, assess the impact of optimizations, and verify system scalability under different load levels. Iterative testing helps organizations identify performance trends, track performance improvements, and ensure continuous optimization of software applications.

In summary, load testing is a critical aspect of performance testing that evaluates how software applications perform under expected and peak load conditions. By understanding the basics of load testing, key concepts, techniques, and best practices, organizations can conduct effective load tests to identify performance bottlenecks, scalability issues, and areas for optimization. Load testing is not just a technical exercise but a strategic endeavor that contributes to the reliability, scalability, and performance of software applications in today's fast-paced and demanding digital landscape.

Stress testing is a crucial aspect of performance testing aimed at evaluating the robustness, resilience, and stability of a software application under extreme load conditions. Next, we delve into stress testing approaches, their significance in software development, techniques, and best practices for conducting effective stress tests.

Importance of Stress Testing: Stress testing helps organizations assess how their software applications perform under extreme load conditions, such as peak user traffic, high transaction volumes, or resource exhaustion scenarios. By subjecting the system to stress conditions, stress testing identifies performance bottlenecks, stability issues, and failure points, enabling organizations to enhance system resilience, reliability, and performance under adverse conditions.

Approaches to Stress Testing: Stress testing can be approached in various ways, each focusing on different aspects of system behavior and performance:

Overload Testing: Overload testing involves subjecting the system to load conditions that exceed its maximum capacity or resource limits. Overload testing helps identify performance bottlenecks, resource exhaustion, and system failures under extreme load conditions, enabling organizations to assess system resilience and scalability.

Command: To simulate overload testing using Apache JMeter, a popular open-source performance testing tool, you can create a test plan with a Thread Group configured to generate a high number of concurrent users or requests exceeding the system's capacity. For example:
bashCopy code

```
./jmeter -n -t your_test_plan.jmx -l your_test_results.jtl
```

Spike Testing: Spike testing evaluates the system's response to sudden spikes or surges in user activity or workload. Spike testing helps assess system stability, scalability, and responsiveness under unexpected load spikes, such as during promotional events, marketing campaigns, or sudden increases in user traffic.

Technique Explanation: To conduct spike testing, you can configure your load testing tool to simulate sudden increases in user activity by rapidly ramping up the number of virtual users or requests. This simulates real-world scenarios where the system experiences sudden spikes in user traffic.

Endurance Testing: Endurance testing, also known as soak testing, assesses the system's performance and stability over an extended period under sustained load conditions. Endurance testing helps identify memory leaks, resource leaks, and degradation in system performance over time, enabling organizations to assess system reliability and stability under prolonged usage.

Best Practices for Stress Testing: To conduct effective stress tests, organizations should follow these best practices:

Identify Critical Scenarios: Identify critical scenarios, use cases, or user interactions that are most likely to cause stress on the system, such as high-traffic pages, complex transactions, or resource-intensive operations. Focus stress testing efforts on these critical scenarios to prioritize testing and maximize test coverage.

Gradual Ramp-up: Gradually ramp up the load during stress testing to simulate realistic load patterns and assess system behavior under increasing load levels. Gradual ramp-up helps prevent sudden spikes in load that may overwhelm the system and distort test results, enabling organizations to identify performance bottlenecks accurately.

Monitor System Health: Continuously monitor system health metrics, such as CPU utilization, memory usage, network bandwidth, and response time, during stress testing. Monitoring system health metrics helps detect performance bottlenecks, resource exhaustion, and system failures in real-time, enabling organizations to take proactive measures to address issues and optimize system performance.

Analyze Performance Data: Analyze performance data collected during stress testing to identify performance bottlenecks, stability issues, and failure points. Use performance monitoring tools and dashboards to visualize performance metrics, identify trends, and prioritize optimization efforts based on data-driven insights.

In summary, stress testing approaches are essential for evaluating the robustness, resilience, and stability of software applications under extreme load conditions. By understanding stress testing approaches, techniques, and best practices, organizations can conduct effective stress tests to identify performance bottlenecks, stability issues, and failure points, enabling them to enhance system resilience, reliability, and performance under adverse conditions. Stress testing is not just a technical exercise but a strategic endeavor that contributes to the overall success and competitiveness of software applications in today's fast-paced and demanding digital landscape.

Chapter 8: Integration Testing Principles

Integration testing is a crucial phase in the software development lifecycle aimed at evaluating the interactions and integration points between different components, modules, or subsystems of a software application. Next, we explore the fundamentals of integration testing, its significance in software development, types of integration testing, techniques, and best practices for conducting effective integration tests.

Importance of Integration Testing: Integration testing plays a vital role in validating the interactions and interfaces between individual components or modules within a software application. By verifying the integration of software components, integration testing helps identify integration issues, data flow errors, interface mismatches, and functional inconsistencies early in the development process, enabling organizations to deliver high-quality, reliable software products to end-users.

Types of Integration Testing: Integration testing can be categorized into several types, each focusing on different levels of integration and testing objectives:

Component Integration Testing: Component integration testing evaluates the interactions and integration of individual software components or modules within the application. It verifies that components interact correctly, exchange data seamlessly, and perform as expected when integrated into the larger system.

Technique Explanation: To conduct component integration testing, developers can use unit testing frameworks such as JUnit for Java or NUnit for .NET to write and execute unit tests for individual components. For example, in a Java project, you can run unit tests using the following Maven command:

bashCopy code

```
mvn test
```

API Integration Testing: API integration testing focuses on testing the interactions and integration of application programming interfaces (APIs) exposed by software components or services. It validates the correctness, functionality, and compatibility of APIs and ensures that they adhere to defined specifications and standards.

Command Example: To perform API integration testing, developers can use tools like Postman or cURL to send HTTP requests to the API endpoints and verify the responses. For example, using cURL to send a GET request to an API endpoint:

bashCopy code

```
curl -X GET https://api.example.com/resource
```

Database Integration Testing: Database integration testing evaluates the interactions and integration of database components within the application. It verifies that database operations, queries, transactions, and data manipulations function correctly, and data is persisted and retrieved accurately from the database.

Deployment Technique: Database integration testing can be performed by deploying a test database instance and executing test scripts or SQL queries to perform database operations and validate data integrity. Continuous integration (CI) pipelines can automate the deployment of test databases and execution of database integration tests.

Best Practices for Integration Testing: To conduct effective integration tests, organizations should follow these best practices:

Define Clear Test Scenarios: Define clear test scenarios, use cases, and test objectives for integration testing based on system requirements, design specifications, and user stories. Clear test scenarios help guide testing efforts, ensure comprehensive test coverage, and prioritize testing activities.

Mock External Dependencies: Use mocking frameworks or stubs to simulate external dependencies, such as third-party APIs, services, or databases, during integration testing. Mocking external dependencies helps isolate components under test, control test environments, and focus testing on specific integration points.

Automate Test Execution: Automate the execution of integration tests using automated testing frameworks, continuous integration (CI) pipelines, or test automation tools. Automated test execution streamlines testing efforts, ensures consistency, repeatability, and scalability of tests, and accelerates feedback cycles in the development process.

Perform Continuous Integration: Integrate integration testing into the continuous integration (CI) process to automate the execution of integration tests as part of the software build and deployment pipeline. Continuous integration ensures that integration tests are executed regularly, detects integration issues early, and facilitates rapid feedback and iteration in the development process.

In summary, integration testing is a critical phase in the software development lifecycle that evaluates the interactions and integration of software components, modules, or subsystems within a software application. By understanding the fundamentals of integration testing, types of integration testing, techniques, and best practices, organizations can conduct effective integration tests to identify integration issues, validate system behavior, and deliver high-quality, reliable software products to end-users. Integration testing is not just a technical task but a strategic endeavor that contributes to the overall success, reliability, and competitiveness of software applications in today's dynamic and competitive marketplace.

Integration testing is a critical phase in the software development lifecycle aimed at verifying the interactions and integration between individual components, modules, or subsystems of a software application. Next, we explore various integration testing strategies, their significance in software development, techniques, and best practices for selecting and implementing effective integration testing strategies.

Significance of Integration Testing Strategies: Integration testing strategies play a vital role in ensuring the reliability, stability, and functionality of software applications by validating the interactions and integration between different components. By defining and implementing appropriate integration testing strategies, organizations can identify integration issues, data flow errors, and interface inconsistencies early in the development process, enabling them to deliver high-quality, robust software products to end-users.

Common Integration Testing Strategies: Integration testing can be approached using different strategies, each focusing on specific aspects of integration and testing objectives:

Top-Down Integration Testing: Top-down integration testing starts with testing the higher-level modules or components first and gradually integrates lower-level modules or components until the entire system is tested. This approach allows for early validation of critical functionalities and interactions at the system level.

Technique Explanation: To perform top-down integration testing, developers can use testing frameworks such as JUnit or NUnit to write and execute integration tests for higher-level modules. For example, in a Java project using JUnit:

bashCopy code

```
mvn test -Dtest=HigherLevelModuleTest
```

Bottom-Up Integration Testing: Bottom-up integration testing begins with testing the lower-level modules or components first and progressively integrates higher-level modules or components until the entire system is tested. This approach allows for early identification and resolution of issues at the component level.

Command Example: For bottom-up integration testing, developers can use testing frameworks or tools to write and execute integration tests for lower-level modules or components. For instance, in a Python project using pytest:

bashCopy code

```
pytest test_lower_level_module.py
```

Big Bang Integration Testing: Big bang integration testing involves integrating all components or modules simultaneously and testing the entire system as a whole. This approach allows for comprehensive validation of system interactions and functionalities but may pose challenges in identifying specific integration issues.

Deployment Technique: To deploy big bang integration testing, developers can use continuous integration (CI) pipelines or automated testing frameworks to integrate all components and execute integration tests. CI tools like Jenkins or GitLab CI can automate the build, integration, and testing process.

Best Practices for Integration Testing Strategies: To select and implement effective integration testing strategies, organizations should follow these best practices:

Understand System Architecture: Gain a thorough understanding of the system architecture, component dependencies, and integration points to identify potential integration issues and determine appropriate testing strategies.

Prioritize Critical Functionalities: Prioritize testing of critical functionalities, high-risk components, and integration points that are essential for system functionality and user experience.

Iterative Testing Approach: Adopt an iterative testing approach to gradually integrate and test components, validate interactions, and identify integration issues early in the development process.

Automate Integration Tests: Automate integration tests using testing frameworks, continuous integration (CI) pipelines, or test automation tools to ensure consistent, repeatable, and scalable testing processes.

In summary, integration testing strategies are essential for validating the interactions and integration between different components, modules, or subsystems within a software application. By understanding various integration testing strategies, techniques, and best practices, organizations can select and implement effective integration testing strategies to identify integration issues, validate system behavior, and deliver high-quality, reliable software products to end-users. Integration testing strategies are not just technical considerations but strategic decisions that contribute to the overall success and competitiveness of software applications in today's dynamic and competitive marketplace.

Chapter 9: Acceptance Testing Best Practices

Acceptance testing is a pivotal phase in the software development lifecycle aimed at validating whether a software application meets the specified requirements and user expectations. Next, we delve into the fundamentals of acceptance testing, its significance in software development, types of acceptance testing, techniques, and best practices for conducting effective acceptance tests.

Significance of Acceptance Testing: Acceptance testing ensures that a software application meets the intended business requirements, functional specifications, and user needs before it is deployed into production. By validating the application from an end-user perspective, acceptance testing helps identify deviations from expected behavior, usability issues, and functional gaps, enabling organizations to deliver high-quality, user-centric software products.

Types of Acceptance Testing: Acceptance testing can be categorized into several types, each focusing on different aspects of software validation and user acceptance:

User Acceptance Testing (UAT): User acceptance testing involves validating the software application's functionality, usability, and performance from the end-user's perspective. It ensures that the application meets user requirements, workflows, and expectations before it is released to production.

Technique Explanation: To conduct user acceptance testing, organizations typically involve end-users or representatives from the target audience who perform predefined test scenarios, tasks, or use cases in a test environment. User acceptance testing can be performed manually or using automated testing tools, depending on the complexity of the application and testing requirements.

Business Acceptance Testing (BAT): Business acceptance testing focuses on verifying that the software application aligns with the organization's business objectives, processes, and regulatory requirements. It ensures that the application supports business operations, complies with industry standards, and delivers tangible business value.

Command Example: To perform business acceptance testing, organizations can define test cases based on business requirements, workflows, and regulatory standards. Test cases are executed in a test environment, and the application's compliance with business requirements is evaluated based on predefined acceptance criteria.

Regulatory Acceptance Testing: Regulatory acceptance testing validates that the software application complies with relevant regulatory standards, industry regulations, and legal requirements. It ensures that the application meets regulatory compliance requirements, data privacy laws, and security standards mandated by regulatory bodies.

Deployment Technique: To deploy regulatory acceptance testing, organizations collaborate with compliance experts, legal advisors, or regulatory agencies to define regulatory requirements, assess application compliance, and validate regulatory controls. Compliance checks, security audits, and penetration testing may be conducted to ensure adherence to regulatory standards.

Best Practices for Acceptance Testing: To conduct effective acceptance tests, organizations should follow these best practices:

Define Clear Acceptance Criteria: Define clear acceptance criteria, test objectives, and success criteria based on business requirements, user needs, and regulatory standards. Clear acceptance criteria help ensure that acceptance tests focus on validating critical functionalities, workflows, and user scenarios.

Involve Stakeholders Early: Involve stakeholders, including end-users, business analysts, product owners, and project sponsors, early in the acceptance testing process. Collaborate with stakeholders to gather requirements, define acceptance criteria, and prioritize test scenarios to ensure alignment with business goals and user expectations.

Use Realistic Test Data: Use realistic test data, scenarios, and environments that closely resemble production conditions during acceptance testing. Realistic test data helps simulate real-world usage scenarios, identify edge cases, and validate application behavior under varying conditions.

Automate Repetitive Tests: Automate repetitive acceptance tests using test automation frameworks, scripting languages, or acceptance testing tools to streamline testing efforts, ensure repeatability, and accelerate test execution. Automated acceptance tests can be integrated into continuous integration (CI) pipelines for regular execution and feedback.

In summary, acceptance testing is a critical phase in the software development lifecycle that validates whether a software application meets the specified requirements, user needs, and business objectives. By understanding the fundamentals of acceptance testing, types of acceptance testing, techniques, and best practices, organizations can conduct effective acceptance tests to ensure that software applications are user-centric, compliant with regulatory standards, and deliver tangible business value. Acceptance testing is not just a technical validation process but a strategic endeavor that contributes to the overall success and competitiveness of software products in today's dynamic and competitive marketplace.

Acceptance criteria serve as the foundation for defining the success criteria and requirements that a software product must meet to gain approval from stakeholders. Next, we explore the significance of acceptance criteria, techniques for defining them effectively, and best practices for ensuring their clarity and relevance in software development projects.

Significance of Acceptance Criteria: Acceptance criteria provide a clear and concise description of the desired functionality, behavior, and characteristics of a software product from the perspective of stakeholders, including end-users, product owners, and project sponsors. By defining acceptance criteria upfront, teams can align their efforts with stakeholder expectations, validate the completeness and correctness of delivered features, and facilitate collaboration and communication throughout the development process.

Techniques for Defining Acceptance Criteria: Several techniques can be employed to define acceptance criteria effectively:

User Stories: Acceptance criteria are often derived from user stories, which describe specific features or functionalities from the perspective of end-users. When writing user stories, acceptance criteria are defined as the conditions that must be met for the user story to be considered complete.

Technique Explanation: To define acceptance criteria using user stories, teams typically follow the "As a [role], I want [feature] so that [benefit]" format, where acceptance criteria are listed as bullet points or checkboxes beneath the user story. For example:

plaintextCopy code

User Story: As a registered user, I want to be able to reset my password, so that I can regain access to my account. Acceptance Criteria: - The reset password link should be sent to the user's email address. - The reset password link should expire after 24 hours. - The user should be able to set a new password using the provided link.

Example Mapping: Example mapping is a collaborative technique that involves gathering stakeholders to brainstorm and discuss concrete examples of desired functionality. Acceptance criteria are derived from these examples, ensuring that they are relevant, concrete, and actionable.

Deployment Technique: To deploy example mapping, teams can schedule a collaborative workshop with stakeholders, including developers, testers, product owners, and domain experts. During the workshop, participants discuss various scenarios and examples related to the feature or functionality under discussion and document acceptance criteria based on these examples.

Behaviour-Driven Development (BDD): BDD is a development methodology that emphasizes collaboration and communication between stakeholders by using natural language specifications to define acceptance criteria. Acceptance criteria are expressed as executable specifications written in a structured, domain-specific language.

Command Example: To define acceptance criteria using BDD, teams can write executable specifications using BDD frameworks such as Cucumber or SpecFlow. For example, in a Cucumber scenario:

plaintextCopy code

Feature: Password Reset Scenario: User resets password Given the user is on the password reset page When the user submits their email address Then the user receives a password reset email And the user can set a new password using the provided link

Best Practices for Defining Acceptance Criteria: To ensure clarity, relevance, and effectiveness of acceptance criteria, teams should follow these best practices:

Collaborate with Stakeholders: Involve stakeholders, including end-users, product owners, and domain experts, in the process of defining acceptance criteria. Collaborative discussions help ensure that acceptance criteria accurately reflect stakeholder expectations and priorities.

Make Acceptance Criteria Specific and Measurable: Ensure that acceptance criteria are specific, measurable, achievable, relevant, and time-bound (SMART). Clearly define the expected outcomes, conditions of satisfaction, and success metrics for each acceptance criterion.

Focus on User Needs and Business Goals: Align acceptance criteria with user needs, business goals, and desired outcomes to ensure that they address the most critical aspects of the software product. Prioritize acceptance criteria based on their impact on user satisfaction and business value.

Keep Acceptance Criteria Agile and Iterative: Acceptance criteria should evolve iteratively throughout the development process based on feedback, changing requirements, and emerging insights. Embrace an agile mindset by continuously refining, updating, and validating acceptance criteria in collaboration with stakeholders.

In summary, acceptance criteria play a crucial role in defining the success criteria and requirements for software products in the eyes of stakeholders. By employing effective techniques such as user stories, example mapping, and behaviour-driven development, teams can define acceptance criteria that are clear, relevant, and actionable. By following best practices and embracing collaboration with stakeholders, teams can ensure that acceptance criteria accurately reflect user needs, business goals, and desired outcomes, thereby driving the successful delivery of high-quality software products. Acceptance criteria definition is not just a documentation exercise but a strategic process that fosters alignment, transparency, and shared understanding across cross-functional teams in software development projects.

Chapter 10: Test Automation Implementation

Test automation is a pivotal aspect of modern software development methodologies, aimed at improving efficiency, reliability, and speed of testing processes. Next, we delve into the fundamentals of test automation, its significance in software development, popular automation tools, techniques, and best practices for implementing successful test automation strategies.

Significance of Test Automation: Test automation involves the use of software tools and scripts to automate the execution of test cases, validation of software functionalities, and verification of expected behaviors. It plays a crucial role in accelerating testing processes, increasing test coverage, and detecting defects early in the development lifecycle. By automating repetitive and time-consuming testing tasks, teams can achieve faster feedback cycles, improve software quality, and deliver products to market more quickly.

Popular Test Automation Tools: Several test automation tools are widely used in the industry to facilitate test automation across various stages of the software development lifecycle:

Selenium: Selenium is a popular open-source framework for automating web browsers. It provides a set of APIs and libraries for interacting with web elements, executing test scripts, and validating web application behavior across different browsers and platforms.

Deployment Technique: To deploy Selenium for test automation, teams can write test scripts using programming languages such as Java, Python, or C#, and use Selenium WebDriver to interact with web elements. For example, to launch a web browser and navigate to a URL using Selenium WebDriver in Java:

bashCopy code

```
java -jar selenium-server-standalone.jar
```

Appium: Appium is an open-source framework for automating mobile applications on iOS, Android, and Windows platforms. It allows testers to write cross-platform test scripts using standard automation APIs, enabling seamless testing of mobile apps across different devices and operating systems.

Command Example: To execute Appium tests for an Android application, testers can set up an Appium server and run test scripts written in languages like Java or Python. For example, to start the Appium server in command-line interface (CLI):

bashCopy code

```
appium
```

JUnit: JUnit is a popular unit testing framework for Java applications. It provides annotations, assertions, and test runners for writing and executing unit tests, enabling developers to automate the testing of individual components and classes in Java applications.

Technique Explanation: To use JUnit for test automation, developers write test methods annotated with JUnit annotations such as **@Test, @Before**, and **@After**. They can then use JUnit test runners to execute the tests and generate test reports. For example, to run JUnit tests from the command line:

bashCopy code

```
java -cp .:junit.jar:hamcrest.jar org.junit.runner.JUnitCore
YourTestClassName
```

Best Practices for Test Automation: To implement successful test automation strategies, teams should follow these best practices:

Identify Suitable Test Cases: Prioritize test cases based on their frequency of execution, complexity, and criticality to the application. Start with automating high-impact test cases that provide maximum test coverage and value.

Maintain Test Suites: Regularly review and update test suites to ensure they remain relevant and effective. Remove obsolete or redundant test cases, refactor test scripts for better maintainability, and enhance test coverage as the application evolves.

Use Version Control: Store test scripts and automation code in version control repositories like Git to track changes, collaborate with team members, and ensure version control of test assets.

Integrate with Continuous Integration: Integrate test automation into continuous integration (CI) pipelines to automate test execution, generate test reports, and provide rapid feedback on code changes. Use CI tools like Jenkins, Travis CI, or GitLab CI for seamless integration of test automation.

Monitor Test Results: Monitor test execution results, identify failing tests, and investigate the root causes of failures promptly. Use test reporting and analytics tools to track test metrics, trends, and quality indicators over time.

In summary, test automation is a fundamental practice in software development that enables teams to streamline testing processes, increase test coverage, and improve software quality. By leveraging popular test automation tools such as Selenium, Appium, and JUnit, teams can automate testing tasks across web, mobile, and desktop applications. By following best practices such as identifying suitable test cases, maintaining test suites, using version control, integrating with continuous integration, and monitoring test results, teams can implement successful test automation strategies and realize the benefits of faster feedback cycles, improved efficiency, and higher-quality software products. Test automation is not just a technical endeavor but a strategic initiative that drives agility, innovation, and competitiveness in today's fast-paced and dynamic software development landscape.

Selecting the right test automation tools is crucial for successful test automation implementation in software development projects. Next, we explore the key considerations, evaluation criteria, and best practices for selecting test automation tools that align with project requirements, technical capabilities, and team preferences.

Importance of Selecting Test Automation Tools: Test automation tools play a significant role in streamlining testing processes, increasing test coverage, and accelerating feedback cycles in software development projects. By selecting the most suitable test automation tools, teams can effectively automate testing tasks, improve software quality, and enhance overall productivity. However, choosing the right tools requires careful evaluation of various factors to ensure compatibility, scalability, and effectiveness.

Key Considerations for Selecting Test Automation Tools: When selecting test automation tools, teams should consider the following key factors:

Project Requirements: Evaluate project requirements, including the type of application (web, mobile, desktop), technologies used (programming languages, frameworks), and testing objectives (functional, regression, performance). Choose test automation tools that support the specific requirements and technical stack of the project.

Tool Features and Capabilities: Assess the features, capabilities, and functionality offered by test automation tools, such as test scripting languages, test frameworks, test reporting, integration with CI/CD pipelines, cross-browser/platform support, and compatibility with testing environments.

Ease of Use and Learning Curve: Consider the ease of use and learning curve associated with test automation tools, especially for team members with varying levels of expertise and experience in test automation. Choose tools that offer intuitive user interfaces, comprehensive documentation, and robust support resources.

Community Support and Ecosystem: Evaluate the level of community support, user community size, and ecosystem surrounding test automation tools, including forums, user groups, online resources, and third-party integrations. Strong community support ensures access to resources, knowledge sharing, and troubleshooting assistance.

Scalability and Maintenance: Consider the scalability and maintenance aspects of test automation tools, including support for large test suites, test data management, test script maintenance, and version control. Choose tools that facilitate scalability, maintainability, and long-term sustainability of test automation efforts.

Evaluation Criteria for Test Automation Tools: To effectively evaluate test automation tools, teams can use the following criteria:

Functionality and Features: Assess the functionality and features offered by test automation tools, including test script creation, test execution, reporting, debugging, and integration capabilities with other tools and frameworks.

Supported Platforms and Technologies: Verify compatibility with target platforms (web browsers, mobile devices, operating systems) and technologies (programming languages, frameworks, databases) to ensure seamless integration and support for diverse testing requirements.

Ease of Integration: Evaluate the ease of integrating test automation tools with existing development and testing infrastructure, including CI/CD pipelines, version control systems, issue tracking tools, and test management platforms.

Cost and Licensing: Consider the cost of test automation tools, including licensing fees, subscription plans, and additional costs for support, training, and maintenance. Compare pricing models and licensing options to determine the most cost-effective solution for the project budget.

Performance and Reliability: Assess the performance, reliability, and stability of test automation tools under different testing scenarios, including large-scale test executions, concurrent user loads, and complex test environments.

Best Practices for Selecting Test Automation Tools: To make informed decisions when selecting test automation tools, teams should follow these best practices:

Define Clear Requirements: Clearly define project requirements, testing objectives, and technical specifications to identify the most suitable test automation tools that meet project needs and align with team capabilities.

Conduct Proof of Concept (POC): Perform proof of concept evaluations for shortlisted test automation tools to validate functionality, features, and compatibility with project requirements. Conduct POCs using real-world use cases and scenarios to assess tool performance and suitability.

Seek Feedback and Recommendations: Gather feedback and recommendations from industry peers, colleagues, and subject matter experts who have experience with test automation tools. Leverage online forums, user groups, and professional networks to solicit recommendations and insights.

Consider Future Needs: Anticipate future needs and requirements for test automation, such as scalability, extensibility, and integration with emerging technologies. Choose test automation tools that can accommodate future growth and evolution of testing practices.

Evaluate Total Cost of Ownership (TCO): Consider the total cost of ownership (TCO) of test automation tools, including initial acquisition costs, ongoing maintenance, training, and support expenses. Calculate TCO over the expected lifespan of the project to assess long-term investment value.

In summary, selecting the right test automation tools is a critical decision that can significantly impact the success of test automation efforts in software development projects. By considering key factors such as project requirements, tool features, ease of use, community support, and scalability, teams can make informed decisions and choose test automation tools that align with project objectives and team capabilities. Following best practices such as defining clear requirements, conducting proof of concept evaluations, seeking feedback, considering future needs, and evaluating total cost of ownership ensures that teams select test automation tools that deliver maximum value and contribute to the overall success of the project. Test automation tool selection is not just a technical decision but a strategic endeavor that requires careful consideration, evaluation, and collaboration to achieve optimal results.

BOOK 2
DEBUGGING PLAYBOOK
MASTERING ERROR LOCALIZATION TECHNIQUES

ROB BOTWRIGHT

Chapter 1: Introduction to System Testing

System testing is a pivotal phase in the software development lifecycle, essential for ensuring the reliability, functionality, and performance of software applications. It encompasses a comprehensive evaluation of the integrated system to validate its compliance with specified requirements and to detect any defects or inconsistencies before deployment. System testing plays a crucial role in identifying defects and vulnerabilities that may have been overlooked during earlier stages of development, such as unit and integration testing. By subjecting the entire system to rigorous testing scenarios, including user interactions, data flows, and integration points, system testing provides assurance that the software meets the expectations of stakeholders and end-users.

System testing is particularly important for complex software systems consisting of multiple components, modules, and subsystems, where individual components may function correctly in isolation but may exhibit unexpected behaviors when integrated together. It verifies the interoperability and compatibility of different system elements, ensuring seamless communication and interaction among them. Through system testing, organizations can mitigate the risks associated with software failures, such as financial losses, reputational damage, and compromised security.

One of the primary objectives of system testing is to validate that the software meets functional requirements specified in the system design and user stories. Test cases are designed to cover various use cases, user workflows, and system functionalities, ensuring that all features operate as intended and deliver the expected outcomes. System testing also assesses non-functional aspects of the software, such as performance, scalability, reliability, and usability, which are critical for delivering a satisfactory user experience.

Automated testing tools and frameworks play a vital role in facilitating system testing by enabling the efficient execution of test cases, the generation of test reports, and the management of test environments. Tools like Selenium, TestNG, and JUnit offer capabilities for automating system tests across different platforms, browsers, and devices, allowing organizations to achieve greater test coverage and accelerate the testing process. By leveraging automation, teams can execute regression tests, smoke tests, and sanity checks repeatedly and consistently, ensuring the stability and robustness of the system across multiple iterations and releases.

In addition to functional and non-functional testing, system testing also encompasses various types of testing, including compatibility testing, usability testing, security testing, and localization testing, depending on the nature of the software and its intended audience. Compatibility testing ensures that the software functions correctly across different operating systems, browsers, and devices, while usability testing assesses the user-friendliness and intuitiveness of the user interface. Security testing focuses on identifying vulnerabilities and weaknesses in the software that could be exploited by malicious actors, protecting sensitive data and ensuring compliance with regulatory requirements. Localization testing verifies that the software is adapted to the linguistic, cultural, and regional preferences of target users, addressing localization issues such as date formats, currency symbols, and language translations.

Effective system testing requires careful planning, execution, and evaluation of test results to identify defects, assess their impact, and prioritize their resolution. Test cases should be designed based on functional requirements, user stories, and acceptance criteria, covering both typical and edge cases to ensure comprehensive test coverage. Test environments should be configured to mimic the production environment as closely as possible, including hardware, software, networks, and configurations, to replicate real-world scenarios accurately.

Continuous integration and continuous delivery (CI/CD) practices further enhance the effectiveness of system testing by enabling the automated deployment of software changes to test environments, the execution of automated tests, and the rapid feedback on code changes. CI/CD pipelines orchestrate the entire software delivery process, from code commit to production deployment, streamlining development workflows and accelerating time-to-market. By integrating system testing into CI/CD pipelines, organizations can achieve faster feedback cycles, higher software quality, and improved collaboration between development and testing teams.

In summary, system testing plays a critical role in ensuring the quality, reliability, and performance of software applications by validating their functionality, interoperability, and compliance with requirements. By subjecting the entire system to rigorous testing scenarios, organizations can identify defects, vulnerabilities, and inconsistencies early in the development lifecycle, reducing the risk of software failures and enhancing user satisfaction. Through a combination of automated testing, comprehensive test coverage, and continuous integration practices, teams can achieve greater efficiency, reliability, and agility in system testing, ultimately delivering high-quality software products that meet the needs of stakeholders and end-users.

Test environments are crucial components of the software development lifecycle, providing dedicated spaces for testing software applications in controlled conditions that replicate real-world scenarios. These environments serve as platforms for executing various types of tests, validating software functionality, and assessing performance, reliability, and security aspects. Understanding the different types of test environments is essential for effectively managing testing activities and ensuring the quality and reliability of software products.

Development Environment: The development environment is where software developers write, compile, and test code before committing changes to version control repositories. It typically consists of individual developer workstations or laptops equipped with development tools, integrated development environments (IDEs), and local development servers. Developers use this environment to experiment with code, implement new features, and troubleshoot issues in a controlled setting.

To set up a development environment, developers install necessary software dependencies, libraries, and development frameworks on their machines using

package managers like npm, pip, or Maven. For example, to install dependencies for a Node.js project using npm:
bashCopy code

```
npm install
```

Testing Environment: The testing environment, also known as the QA environment or staging environment, is where software testers conduct various types of tests to validate software functionality, performance, and compatibility. It closely resembles the production environment in terms of hardware, software configurations, network infrastructure, and data, allowing testers to simulate real-world conditions and scenarios.

To deploy an application to a testing environment, testers use deployment tools or scripts to package the application files and deploy them to dedicated testing servers or cloud-based environments. For example, to deploy a web application using Docker containers:
bashCopy code

```
docker-compose up -d
```

Integration Environment: The integration environment is where developers and testers integrate individual software components, modules, or services to validate their interoperability and compatibility. It facilitates integration testing, where teams verify that different parts of the system work together seamlessly and exchange data correctly.

To set up an integration environment, teams deploy the integrated components to a shared environment or containerized infrastructure, configure communication channels, and execute integration tests. Continuous integration (CI) tools like Jenkins or GitLab CI automate the process of deploying and testing integrated components. For example, to trigger an integration test job in Jenkins:

bashCopy code

jenkins-cli build integration-test-job

User Acceptance Testing (UAT) Environment: The UAT environment is where stakeholders, end-users, or client representatives validate the software against business requirements, user stories, and acceptance criteria. It serves as the final stage of testing before software is deployed to production, allowing users to verify that the software meets their needs and expectations.

To prepare a UAT environment, testers deploy the tested software to a dedicated environment accessible to stakeholders, configure user accounts, permissions, and test data, and provide user documentation and training materials. Stakeholders then execute predefined test cases and scenarios to evaluate the software's usability, functionality, and compliance with business objectives.

Production Environment: The production environment is where the software is deployed and made available to end-users for regular use. It represents the live or operational environment where the software interacts with real users, data, and external systems. Maintaining the stability, availability, and security of the production environment is critical to ensuring uninterrupted service and user satisfaction.

To deploy software to a production environment, organizations follow established deployment processes and procedures, such as blue-green deployments, canary releases, or rolling updates. Deployment automation tools like Ansible, Puppet, or Chef automate the deployment process and ensure consistency across production environments. For example, to deploy a new version of an application using Ansible:

bashCopy code

ansible-playbook deploy.yml

Disaster Recovery (DR) Environment: The disaster recovery environment is a standby environment designed to ensure business continuity and data protection in the event of a catastrophic failure or outage in the production environment. It contains redundant infrastructure, backup systems, and data replication mechanisms to minimize downtime and data loss.

To maintain a disaster recovery environment, organizations replicate data and infrastructure components from the production environment to a secondary location, such as a remote data center or cloud region. Continuous data replication, automated failover mechanisms, and periodic disaster recovery drills help ensure the readiness and effectiveness of the DR environment in mitigating potential risks and disruptions.

Each type of test environment serves a specific purpose in the software development and testing lifecycle, providing dedicated spaces for executing different types of tests, validating software functionality, and ensuring the quality, reliability, and security of software applications. By understanding the characteristics, requirements, and deployment strategies of each test environment, organizations can effectively manage testing activities, minimize risks, and deliver high-quality software products to end-users.

Chapter 2: Understanding Test Environments

Test environments are integral components of the software development lifecycle, providing dedicated spaces for testing software applications under controlled conditions that replicate real-world scenarios. These environments serve as platforms for executing various types of tests, validating software functionality, and assessing performance, reliability, and security aspects. Understanding the different types of test environments is essential for effectively managing testing activities and ensuring the quality and reliability of software products.

Development Environment: The development environment is where software developers write, compile, and test code before committing changes to version control repositories. It typically consists of individual developer workstations or laptops equipped with development tools, integrated development environments (IDEs), and local development servers. Developers use this environment to experiment with code, implement new features, and troubleshoot issues in a controlled setting.

To set up a development environment, developers install necessary software dependencies, libraries, and development frameworks on their machines using package managers like npm, pip, or Maven. For example, to install dependencies for a Node.js project using npm:

bashCopy code

```
npm install
```

Testing Environment: The testing environment, also known as the QA environment or staging environment, is where software testers conduct various types of tests to validate software functionality, performance, and compatibility. It closely resembles the production environment in terms of hardware, software configurations, network infrastructure, and data, allowing testers to simulate real-world conditions and scenarios.

To deploy an application to a testing environment, testers use deployment tools or scripts to package the application files and deploy them to dedicated testing servers or cloud-based environments. For example, to deploy a web application using Docker containers:

bashCopy code

```
docker-compose up -d
```

Integration Environment: The integration environment is where developers and testers integrate individual software components, modules, or services to validate their interoperability and compatibility. It facilitates integration testing, where teams verify that different parts of the system work together seamlessly and exchange data correctly.

To set up an integration environment, teams deploy the integrated components to a shared environment or containerized infrastructure, configure communication channels, and execute integration tests. Continuous integration (CI) tools like Jenkins or GitLab CI automate the process of deploying and testing integrated components. For example, to trigger an integration test job in Jenkins:

bashCopy code

```
jenkins-cli build integration-test-job
```

User Acceptance Testing (UAT) Environment: The UAT environment is where stakeholders, end-users, or client representatives validate the software against business requirements, user stories, and acceptance criteria. It serves as the final stage of testing before software is deployed to production, allowing users to verify that the software meets their needs and expectations.

To prepare a UAT environment, testers deploy the tested software to a dedicated environment accessible to stakeholders, configure user accounts, permissions, and test data, and provide user documentation and training materials. Stakeholders then execute predefined test cases and scenarios to evaluate the software's usability, functionality, and compliance with business objectives.

Production Environment: The production environment is where the software is deployed and made available to end-users for regular use. It represents the live or operational environment where the software interacts with real users, data, and external systems. Maintaining the stability, availability, and security of the production environment is critical to ensuring uninterrupted service and user satisfaction.

To deploy software to a production environment, organizations follow established deployment processes and procedures, such as blue-green deployments, canary releases, or rolling updates. Deployment automation tools like Ansible, Puppet, or Chef automate the deployment process and ensure consistency across production environments. For example, to deploy a new version of an application using Ansible:

bashCopy code

```
ansible-playbook deploy.yml
```

Disaster Recovery (DR) Environment: The disaster recovery environment is a standby environment designed to ensure business continuity and data protection in the event of a catastrophic failure or outage in the production environment. It contains redundant infrastructure, backup systems, and data replication mechanisms to minimize downtime and data loss.

To maintain a disaster recovery environment, organizations replicate data and infrastructure components from the production environment to a secondary location, such as a remote data center or cloud region. Continuous data replication, automated failover mechanisms, and periodic disaster recovery drills help ensure the readiness and effectiveness of the DR environment in mitigating potential risks and disruptions.

Each type of test environment serves a specific purpose in the software development and testing lifecycle, providing dedicated spaces for executing different types of tests, validating software functionality, and ensuring the quality, reliability, and security of software applications. By understanding the characteristics, requirements, and deployment strategies of each test environment, organizations can effectively manage testing activities, minimize risks, and deliver high-quality software products to end-users.

Setting up test environments is a critical aspect of software development and testing, providing dedicated spaces for validating software functionality, performance, and reliability under controlled conditions that replicate real-world scenarios. These environments serve as platforms for executing various types of tests, including unit tests, integration tests, regression tests, and user acceptance tests, enabling teams to identify defects, assess quality, and ensure the readiness of software products for production deployment.

Identifying Test Environment Requirements: Before setting up test environments, it's essential to identify and understand the specific requirements for testing different aspects of the software. This includes defining the hardware and software configurations, network infrastructure, test data, and access controls needed to support testing activities effectively. By documenting test environment requirements, teams can ensure that the environments are properly configured to meet the needs of testing processes and objectives.

Selecting Test Environment Tools and Technologies: Once the requirements are defined, teams can select appropriate tools and technologies for setting up test environments. This may include virtualization platforms, containerization technologies, configuration management tools, and deployment automation frameworks that streamline the provisioning, configuration, and management of test environments. Tools like Docker, Kubernetes, Vagrant, and Terraform are commonly used for creating and managing test environments efficiently.

To create a test environment using Docker, for example, teams can define a Dockerfile specifying the software dependencies and configurations required for testing, then build and run Docker containers based on the Dockerfile. Here's an example Dockerfile for setting up a test environment for a Node.js application:

dockerfileCopy code

```
FROM node:latest WORKDIR /app COPY package.json .
RUN npm install COPY . . EXPOSE 3000 CMD ["npm",
"start"]
```

To build and run the Docker container:
bashCopy code

```
docker build -t my-node-app . docker run -d -p 3000:3000
my-node-app
```

Creating Test Data and Test Scenarios: In addition to configuring the test environment infrastructure, teams need to prepare test data and define test scenarios that cover various use cases, edge cases, and user workflows. Test data should include representative datasets, input parameters, and conditions that exercise different features and functionalities of the software. Test scenarios outline step-by-step procedures for executing tests, including preconditions, actions, expected results, and validation criteria.

Provisioning Test Environments: Once the test environment infrastructure is defined and configured, teams can provision the necessary resources and deploy the software under test to the test environments. This may involve setting up virtual machines, containers, or cloud instances with the required hardware and software configurations, installing and configuring the software components, and deploying application artifacts, databases, and middleware.

Automated deployment tools and scripts play a crucial role in streamlining the provisioning process, enabling teams to automate the deployment of software to test environments consistently. Tools like Ansible, Puppet, Chef, and SaltStack provide infrastructure as code (IaC) capabilities for automating infrastructure provisioning and configuration management tasks.

For example, to use Ansible for provisioning test environments, teams can define Ansible playbooks that describe the desired state of the test environment and the tasks needed to achieve that state. Here's an example Ansible playbook for setting up a test environment for a web application:

yamlCopy code

```
--- - name: Provision Test Environment hosts: test_servers tasks: - name: Install Apache HTTP Server yum: name: httpd state: present - name: Copy Web Application Files copy: src: /path/to/webapp dest: /var/www/html - name: Start Apache Service service: name: httpd state: started enabled: yes
```

To execute the Ansible playbook:

bashCopy code

```
ansible-playbook provision.yml
```

Configuring Test Environment Monitoring and Management: After setting up test environments, teams should establish monitoring and management mechanisms to track the health, performance, and availability of the environments and troubleshoot any issues that arise during testing. This may involve implementing monitoring tools, logging solutions, and alerting systems that provide real-time visibility into the state of test environments and notify stakeholders of any anomalies or incidents.

Tools like Nagios, Prometheus, Grafana, and ELK Stack are commonly used for monitoring and logging test environment metrics, such as CPU usage, memory consumption, disk I/O, network traffic, and application logs. By proactively monitoring test environments, teams can identify performance bottlenecks, resource constraints, and configuration errors that may impact testing activities and take corrective actions to mitigate risks and ensure the reliability of test environments.

Setting up test environments requires careful planning, configuration, and automation to ensure that the environments are properly provisioned, configured, and managed to support testing activities effectively. By following best practices for defining requirements, selecting tools and technologies, creating test data and scenarios, provisioning resources, and monitoring environments, teams can establish robust test environments that facilitate thorough testing and validation of software products, leading to improved quality, reliability, and customer satisfaction.

Chapter 3: Test Case Development

Writing effective test cases is a crucial aspect of software testing, enabling testers to systematically verify the functionality, behavior, and performance of software applications. Effective test cases are well-defined, comprehensive, and targeted, covering various use cases, scenarios, and edge cases to ensure thorough test coverage and validate software requirements and user expectations. By following best practices for writing test cases, testers can improve the efficiency, effectiveness, and reliability of testing processes, leading to higher software quality and reduced defects in production releases.

Understanding Requirements and Use Cases: Before writing test cases, testers need to understand the software requirements, user stories, and use cases that define the desired behavior and functionality of the software. By analyzing requirements documents, user stories, and acceptance criteria, testers can identify the key features, workflows, and scenarios that need to be tested. This understanding helps testers prioritize test cases and focus on critical functionalities and user journeys.

Identifying Test Scenarios and Test Conditions: Based on the requirements and use cases, testers identify test scenarios and test conditions that represent different aspects of the software's functionality and behavior. Test scenarios outline the steps, actions, and inputs required to validate specific features or workflows, while test conditions specify the preconditions, input data, and expected outcomes for each test scenario. Testers should consider various factors, such as boundary conditions, error handling, and performance constraints, when defining test conditions.

Writing Clear and Concise Test Steps: Effective test cases consist of clear and concise test steps that describe the actions to be performed, the input data to be provided, and the expected outcomes to be observed. Test steps should be written in a simple, unambiguous language that is easy to understand and execute. Each test step should focus on a single action or verification point, avoiding ambiguity or multiple assertions within a single step.

Including Preconditions and Postconditions: Test cases should include preconditions that specify the initial state or setup required for executing the test, such as system configurations, data prerequisites, or user permissions. Similarly, postconditions describe the expected state or outcomes after the test execution, such as database updates, user interface changes, or error messages. Including preconditions and postconditions helps ensure that tests are executed consistently and reliably.

Adding Data and Input Variations: To validate software behavior under different conditions, test cases should include variations in input data, parameters, and configurations. Testers should consider boundary values, edge cases, and invalid inputs to ensure thorough test coverage and identify potential defects or vulnerabilities. Using data-driven testing techniques, testers can execute test cases with multiple datasets or input values to validate software behavior across different scenarios.

Verifying Expected Outcomes and Assertions: Each test case should include assertions or verification points that validate the expected outcomes or results of the test. Assertions compare the actual outcomes observed during test execution with the expected outcomes specified in the test case, flagging any discrepancies or deviations as test failures. Testers should define explicit success criteria and acceptance criteria for each test case, ensuring that tests accurately reflect the intended behavior of the software.

Organizing Test Cases for Reusability and Maintainability: Test cases should be organized and structured in a logical and systematic manner to facilitate reuse, maintenance, and scalability. Test suites or test modules can group related test cases based on functional areas, features, or user stories, making it easier to manage and execute tests. Test case templates or standardized formats can standardize the writing style and conventions used in test cases, promoting consistency and clarity across testing efforts.

Reviewing and Validating Test Cases: Before executing test cases, testers should review and validate them to ensure accuracy, completeness, and relevance. Test case reviews involve peer reviews or walkthroughs where testers, developers, and other stakeholders review test cases for correctness, clarity, and alignment with requirements. Validation involves executing test cases against the software under test to verify that they produce the expected outcomes and detect any defects or issues.

By following these best practices for writing effective test cases, testers can enhance the quality, reliability, and effectiveness of software testing efforts, leading to improved software quality, faster defect detection, and increased confidence in the software's functionality and performance. Effective test cases serve as valuable assets throughout the software development lifecycle, providing a systematic and structured approach to validating software requirements, identifying defects, and ensuring the delivery of high-quality software products to end-users.

Test case management is a critical component of software testing, encompassing the creation, organization, execution, and analysis of test cases to ensure thorough validation of software functionality and behavior. Effective test case management involves the systematic planning, design, documentation, execution, and tracking of test cases throughout the software development lifecycle, enabling testers to efficiently validate software requirements, identify defects, and ensure the quality and reliability of software products.

Test Case Planning and Design: Test case management begins with the planning and design phase, where testers define the scope, objectives, and approach for testing specific features or functionalities of the software. Testers collaborate with stakeholders to gather requirements, analyze user stories, and identify test scenarios that cover various use cases, workflows, and edge cases. Using test case management tools or templates, testers document test case specifications, including test steps, expected outcomes, preconditions, and postconditions.

To create test cases using a test case management tool like TestRail, testers can log in to the TestRail web interface, navigate to the project dashboard, and click on the "Add Test Case" button. They can then enter details such as the test case title, description, steps, expected results, and associated requirements or user stories. TestRail allows testers to organize test cases into test suites, assign priority and severity levels, and link test cases to corresponding test plans and test runs.

Organizing Test Cases and Test Suites: Once test cases are created, testers organize them into logical groupings or test suites based on functional areas, features, or user stories. Test suites help testers categorize and manage test cases effectively, making it easier to prioritize, execute, and track tests across different testing efforts. Testers can create hierarchical test suites and sub-suites to represent the hierarchical structure of the software under test and align test cases with specific modules or components.

To organize test cases into test suites using TestRail, testers can create new test suites from the project dashboard, assign descriptive names or labels to the test suites, and drag and drop test cases into the appropriate suites. TestRail allows testers to customize the test suite hierarchy, reorder test cases within suites, and group related test suites into larger test plans for comprehensive test coverage.

Test Case Execution and Reporting: After organizing test cases, testers execute them against the software under test to validate its functionality, behavior, and performance. Test case execution involves following the predefined test steps, inputting test data, and verifying the actual outcomes against the expected results specified in the test cases. Testers record test results, including pass/fail statuses, observations, and comments, in the test case management tool to track progress and document defects.

To execute test cases using a test case management tool like TestRail, testers can create test runs within the test plan corresponding to the current testing cycle or sprint. They can assign test runs to individual testers or testing teams, specify the target environments or configurations for testing, and schedule test runs for execution. Testers execute test cases by selecting the appropriate test run, navigating to the test case details, and marking the test results based on the observed outcomes.

Defect Management and Traceability: During test case execution, testers may encounter defects or issues that deviate from the expected behavior of the software. Test case management tools facilitate defect management by allowing testers to report, track, and prioritize defects within the same platform used for managing test cases. Testers can create defect reports, including detailed descriptions, steps to reproduce, and screenshots or attachments, and link them to the corresponding test cases for traceability.

To report defects using TestRail, testers can log in to the defect tracking module, create a new defect report, and enter relevant details such as the defect title, description, severity, and priority. TestRail provides integration with popular defect tracking systems like Jira, Bugzilla, and Redmine, allowing testers to synchronize defect information between TestRail and the external defect tracking system. Testers can link defects to specific test cases, test runs, or requirements, enabling traceability and impact analysis.

Test Case Maintenance and Versioning: As the software evolves through multiple iterations or releases, test cases may need to be updated, refined, or expanded to accommodate changes in requirements, features, or user stories. Test case management tools support test case maintenance and versioning by providing version control mechanisms, audit trails, and history tracking capabilities. Testers can revise existing test cases, add new test cases, or retire obsolete test cases while maintaining a complete record of changes.

To update test cases using TestRail, testers can navigate to the test case details, make the necessary modifications to the test steps, expected results, or other attributes, and save the changes. TestRail automatically tracks version history for each test case, allowing testers to view previous revisions, compare versions, and revert to earlier versions if needed. Testers can also archive or deactivate outdated test cases to declutter the test case repository and improve manageability.

Continuous Improvement and Optimization: Test case management is an iterative process that involves continuous improvement and optimization based on feedback, lessons learned, and best practices. Testers collaborate with stakeholders to review testing processes, identify areas for improvement, and implement corrective actions or enhancements to streamline test case management workflows. Testers leverage analytics and metrics provided by test case management tools to measure test coverage, defect density, and testing efficiency and make data-driven decisions to optimize testing efforts.

By adopting a systematic approach to test case management and leveraging the capabilities of test case management tools, testers can streamline testing processes, improve collaboration, and enhance the quality and reliability of software products. Test case management serves as a cornerstone of software testing, providing a structured framework for planning, executing, and tracking tests, and ensuring that software meets quality standards, regulatory requirements, and user expectations.

Chapter 4: Test Execution and Reporting

Test execution process is a crucial phase in software testing, involving the systematic execution of test cases to validate the functionality, behavior, and performance of software applications. Test execution encompasses the steps of preparing test environments, executing test cases, recording test results, and analyzing test outcomes to identify defects, assess quality, and ensure the readiness of software for production deployment. Effective test execution requires careful planning, coordination, and execution of test cases across different testing cycles, environments, and configurations to achieve comprehensive test coverage and validate software requirements and user expectations.

Preparation of Test Environments: Before initiating test execution, testers need to ensure that test environments are properly configured, provisioned, and prepared to support testing activities. This involves setting up hardware, software, and network infrastructure components according to test environment specifications and requirements. Testers deploy the software under test to test environments, configure test data, and establish connectivity with external systems or dependencies. Automated deployment tools and scripts can streamline the preparation process by automating infrastructure provisioning, software deployment, and configuration management tasks.

To deploy a web application to a test environment using a deployment script, testers can execute the following CLI command:

bashCopy code

./deploy.sh test-environment

This command runs the deployment script named "deploy.sh" and specifies the target test environment as an argument, triggering the deployment of the application to the specified environment.

Execution of Test Cases: Once test environments are set up and configured, testers proceed to execute test cases against the software under test. Test execution involves following the predefined test steps, inputting test data, and verifying the actual outcomes against the expected results specified in the test cases. Testers may execute test cases manually or use automated testing tools to automate test execution and accelerate testing cycles. Testers log test results, including pass/fail statuses, observations, and comments, to document test execution progress and track defects.

To execute a specific test suite using a test automation tool like Selenium WebDriver, testers can run the following CLI command:

bashCopy code

selenium-runner execute test-suite.xml

This command triggers the execution of the test suite specified in the XML file named "test-suite.xml" using Selenium WebDriver, executing the defined test cases and generating test execution reports.

Recording Test Results: During test execution, testers record test results to document the outcomes of individual test cases and overall test runs. Test results include pass/fail statuses, error messages, screenshots, and log files that provide insights into the behavior and performance of the software under test. Testers log test results in test case management tools or test execution frameworks, enabling stakeholders to review test outcomes, track defects, and make informed decisions about the software's quality and readiness for release.

To record test results in a test case management tool like TestRail, testers can use the following CLI command to submit test results for a specific test run:

bashCopy code

```
testrail submit-results --run-id 123 --results results.json
```

This command submits the test results stored in a JSON file named "results.json" to the test run identified by the ID "123" in TestRail, updating the test run with the latest execution outcomes and statuses.

Defect Identification and Reporting: During test execution, testers may encounter defects or issues that deviate from the expected behavior of the software. Testers identify defects by analyzing test results, logs, error messages, and user feedback, and report them using defect tracking systems or bug tracking tools. Defect reports include detailed descriptions, steps to reproduce, severity levels, and priority ratings, enabling developers to investigate and resolve defects efficiently.

To report a defect using a defect tracking system like Jira, testers can use the following CLI command to create a new defect report:

bashCopy code

```
jira create-issue --project "PROJ" --type "Bug" --summary "Defect in Feature X" --description "Detailed description of the defect..."
```

This command creates a new defect report in the specified Jira project ("PROJ") with the type "Bug" and provides a summary and description of the defect.

Analysis of Test Outcomes: After completing test execution, testers analyze test outcomes to assess the quality, reliability, and readiness of the software for production deployment. Test analysis involves reviewing test results, identifying patterns or trends in defects, assessing test coverage, and evaluating the effectiveness of test cases and testing strategies. Testers collaborate with stakeholders to prioritize defects, plan regression testing, and make data-driven decisions about the software's release readiness.

To analyze test outcomes and generate test reports using a test management tool like Zephyr, testers can run the following CLI command to export test results and metrics:

bashCopy code

```
zephyr export-results --project "PROJ" --test-cycle "Release 1.0" --format "PDF" --output "test-report.pdf"
```

This command exports test results and metrics from the specified test cycle ("Release 1.0") in the project ("PROJ") to a PDF file named "test-report.pdf," providing stakeholders with insights into test execution progress and quality metrics.

By following a systematic test execution process and leveraging automation tools and techniques, testers can efficiently validate software functionality, identify defects, and ensure the quality and reliability of software products. Effective test execution is essential for delivering high-quality software that meets user requirements, complies with industry standards, and delivers value to stakeholders.

Test reporting and analysis are integral components of the software testing process, involving the systematic collection, documentation, and interpretation of test results to evaluate the quality, effectiveness, and readiness of software applications for deployment. Test reporting entails the generation of comprehensive reports summarizing test execution outcomes, defect metrics, and testing progress, providing stakeholders with insights into the software's stability, reliability, and compliance with requirements. Test analysis, on the other hand, involves the examination of test data, trends, and patterns to identify areas for improvement, assess test coverage, and prioritize defects for resolution, enabling teams to make informed decisions and optimize testing strategies for future releases.

Generation of Test Reports: Test reporting begins with the generation of test reports that capture key metrics, findings, and observations from test execution activities. Test reports serve as communication tools, enabling testers to convey test results, progress, and quality metrics to project stakeholders, including developers, product managers, and business analysts. Test reports typically include summaries of test execution results, defect metrics, test coverage statistics, and any pertinent observations or recommendations for further action.

To generate test reports using a test management tool like TestRail, testers can use the following CLI command to export test results and metrics to a report format:

bashCopy code

```
testrail export-results --project "PROJ" --test-run "Release 1.0" --format "PDF" --output "test-report.pdf"
```

This command exports test results and metrics from the specified test run ("Release 1.0") in the project ("PROJ") to a PDF file named "test-report.pdf," providing stakeholders with a comprehensive overview of test execution outcomes and quality metrics.

Analysis of Test Metrics: Once test reports are generated, testers analyze test metrics to gain insights into the software's quality, stability, and compliance with requirements. Test metrics include various quantitative and qualitative indicators, such as defect density, test coverage, pass/fail ratios, and mean time to failure (MTTF), which help assess the effectiveness of testing efforts and identify areas for improvement. Testers examine trends in test metrics over time, comparing current results with historical data to identify patterns and deviations.

To analyze test metrics using a test management tool like Zephyr, testers can use the following CLI command to retrieve test metrics data and visualize it in a dashboard:

bashCopy code

```
zephyr get-metrics --project "PROJ" --test-cycle "Release 1.0" --format "JSON" --output "test-metrics.json"
```

This command retrieves test metrics data for the specified test cycle ("Release 1.0") in the project ("PROJ") in JSON format and saves it to a file named "test-metrics.json," allowing testers to analyze and interpret test metrics using visualization tools or custom scripts.

Identification of Defect Trends: In addition to test metrics, testers analyze defect data to identify trends, patterns, and common root causes contributing to software defects. By examining defect trends over multiple test cycles or releases, testers can pinpoint recurring issues, prioritize defect resolution efforts, and implement preventive measures to mitigate similar defects in the future. Testers categorize defects based on severity, priority, and impact, facilitating risk-based decision-making and resource allocation.

To identify defect trends using a defect tracking system like Jira, testers can use the following CLI command to query defect data and generate a trend analysis report:

bashCopy code

```
jira query-issues --project "PROJ" --type "Bug" --status "Resolved" --created-after "2023-01-01" --output "defect-trends.csv"
```

This command queries the Jira database for resolved defects ("Bug" type) in the specified project ("PROJ") created after January 1, 2023, and exports the query results to a CSV file named "defect-trends.csv," allowing testers to perform trend analysis and identify patterns in defect resolution.

Root Cause Analysis: To address recurring defects and improve software quality, testers conduct root cause analysis to identify underlying factors contributing to defect occurrence. Root cause analysis involves investigating the circumstances, conditions, and actions leading to defect manifestation, uncovering systemic issues, process deficiencies, or environmental factors affecting software stability and reliability. Testers collaborate with cross-functional teams to implement corrective actions and preventive measures addressing root causes and enhancing software quality assurance practices.

To perform root cause analysis using a collaborative tool like Confluence, testers can use the following CLI command to create a root cause analysis document and share it with team members:

bashCopy code

```
confluence create-document --space "SPACE" --title "Root Cause Analysis Report" --template "Root Cause Analysis" --output "root-cause-analysis.docx"
```

This command creates a new root cause analysis document in the specified Confluence space ("SPACE") using a predefined template named "Root Cause Analysis" and exports the document to a Word file named "root-cause-analysis.docx," facilitating collaboration and knowledge sharing among team members.

Continuous Improvement Initiatives: Based on test reporting and analysis findings, teams initiate continuous improvement initiatives to enhance testing processes, methodologies, and tools for better software quality assurance outcomes. Continuous improvement involves iteratively refining testing practices, optimizing test automation frameworks, and adopting emerging technologies and best practices to streamline testing workflows, increase testing efficiency, and deliver high-quality software products that meet user expectations and business objectives.

To initiate a continuous improvement initiative using a project management tool like Trello, testers can use the following CLI command to create a new improvement project board and add improvement tasks:

bashCopy code

```
trello create-board --name "Continuous Improvement Project" --organization "ORG" --output "improvement-board"
```

This command creates a new project board named "Continuous Improvement Project" within the specified organization ("ORG") in Trello and generates a link to the board, allowing testers to track improvement tasks, assign responsibilities, and monitor progress towards quality improvement goals.

By leveraging test reporting and analysis techniques, testers can gain valuable insights into the quality and reliability of software applications, enabling them to make informed decisions, prioritize testing efforts, and drive continuous improvement initiatives to deliver high-quality software products that meet user needs and exceed expectations. Test reporting and analysis serve as essential components of the software testing process, providing stakeholders with visibility into testing progress, defect trends, and quality metrics, and facilitating data-driven decision-making and risk management throughout the software development lifecycle.

Chapter 5: Regression Testing Techniques

Overview of regression testing is a fundamental aspect of software testing, involving the systematic re-execution of previously validated test cases to ensure that recent changes or enhancements to the software have not introduced new defects or adversely impacted existing functionality. Regression testing aims to verify the stability and integrity of software across successive iterations or releases by detecting and mitigating regression defects that may arise due to code modifications, configuration changes, or integration updates. This comprehensive examination of the software's behavior helps maintain software quality, reliability, and user satisfaction by identifying and addressing potential regressions before they impact end-users or disrupt business operations.

Understanding Regression Testing: Regression testing is a quality assurance technique used to validate software changes and modifications while safeguarding against unintended side effects or regressions that may occur as a result of these changes. It involves re-executing a subset of existing test cases or test suites to ensure that the software behaves as expected after modifications, updates, or enhancements are made. Regression testing helps mitigate the risk of regression defects, which are defects that reappear or are introduced due to changes made to the software codebase or configuration.

Types of Regression Testing: There are several types of regression testing, each serving specific purposes and objectives within the software development lifecycle. These include:

Unit Regression Testing: Focuses on validating individual units or components of the software to ensure that recent code changes have not introduced defects or broken existing functionality.

Integration Regression Testing: Verifies the interaction and integration between different modules, components, or systems to detect any issues arising from changes in interfaces or dependencies.

Functional Regression Testing: Validates the functional behavior of the software by re-executing functional test cases to verify that recent changes have not affected core functionality or user workflows.

Non-Functional Regression Testing: Ensures that non-functional aspects such as performance, security, usability, and compatibility remain unaffected by software changes.

Selective Regression Testing: Focuses on retesting only those areas of the software that are likely to be affected by recent changes, optimizing test coverage and execution time.

Regression Testing Process: The regression testing process involves several key steps, including test selection, test prioritization, test execution, defect identification, and regression test suite maintenance. Test selection involves identifying a subset of existing test cases that are relevant to the changes being made and prioritizing them based on factors such as criticality, risk, and impact. Test execution entails re-executing selected test cases against the modified software to detect any regressions or deviations from expected behavior. Defects identified during regression testing are logged, prioritized, and addressed by developers, and fixes are verified through subsequent regression testing cycles. Regression test suites are continuously updated and maintained to reflect changes in software requirements, features, and functionalities.

Automation of Regression Testing: Automation plays a crucial role in regression testing by enabling the rapid and efficient execution of regression test suites, especially in large and complex software projects with frequent code changes. Test automation tools such as Selenium WebDriver, TestNG, JUnit, and NUnit automate the execution of regression test cases, allowing testers to execute tests across different platforms, browsers, and configurations with minimal manual intervention. Automated regression testing helps accelerate testing cycles, improve test coverage, and detect regressions early in the development process, leading to faster feedback loops and reduced time-to-market.

Regression Testing Best Practices: To maximize the effectiveness and efficiency of regression testing, organizations should adhere to best practices and guidelines, including:

Regular Regression Testing: Conduct regression testing regularly throughout the software development lifecycle, ideally after each code change, build, or release.

Test Case Maintenance: Keep regression test suites up-to-date by reviewing, updating, and retiring obsolete test cases to ensure relevance and accuracy.

Test Environment Management: Maintain stable and consistent test environments to minimize environmental variations and ensure reliable test results.

Version Control: Use version control systems such as Git or SVN to track changes to test assets, including test cases, scripts, and configurations.

Collaboration and Communication: Foster collaboration between development, testing, and other stakeholders to align regression testing efforts with project timelines, priorities, and goals.

Continuous Integration and Deployment: Integrate regression testing into continuous integration and deployment pipelines to automate test execution and feedback loops.

Challenges of Regression Testing: Despite its importance, regression testing poses several challenges, including:

Test Suite Maintenance: Managing large and complex regression test suites requires ongoing maintenance and optimization to ensure efficiency and relevance.

Resource Constraints: Limited time, budget, and resources may hinder the thoroughness and frequency of regression testing efforts.

Test Environment Dependencies: Dependencies on external systems, databases, or third-party services can complicate regression testing and introduce variability.

Test Data Management: Generating and managing test data for regression testing can be challenging, particularly for scenarios involving large datasets or complex data dependencies.

Test Oracles: Identifying suitable test oracles or expected outcomes for regression tests can be difficult, especially for non-deterministic or poorly defined requirements.

Despite these challenges, effective regression testing is essential for ensuring software quality, reliability, and user satisfaction. By implementing regression testing processes, tools, and best practices, organizations can minimize the risk of regression defects, optimize testing efforts, and deliver high-quality software products that meet user expectations and business objectives.

Regression test selection techniques are vital strategies employed in software testing to optimize testing efforts by selectively re-executing relevant test cases from the existing test suite, thus ensuring that software changes do not introduce unintended side effects or regressions. These techniques aim to minimize testing time and resource utilization while maximizing the effectiveness of regression testing, which is essential for maintaining software quality and stability across successive releases or updates. By intelligently selecting a subset of test cases based on factors such as code changes, impacted functionalities, and risk assessment, regression test selection techniques enable organizations to achieve efficient test coverage and expedite the release cycle without compromising quality.

Code Coverage-Based Selection: Code coverage-based regression test selection techniques focus on identifying and prioritizing test cases that exercise code affected by recent changes or modifications. These techniques leverage code coverage metrics, such as statement coverage, branch coverage, and path coverage, to determine the impact of code changes on the existing test suite. By analyzing the code changes using version control systems like Git and performing code coverage analysis using tools like JaCoCo or Cobertura, testers can identify the portions of code that require regression testing and selectively execute relevant test cases to verify the correctness and stability of the modified code.

bashCopy code

```
git diff <commit1>..<commit2> --name-only
```

This command compares two commits (<commit1> and <commit2>) in a Git repository and lists the files that have been modified between the two commits, helping testers identify the code changes that need regression testing.

Impact Analysis-Based Selection: Impact analysis-based regression test selection techniques assess the impact of software changes on the existing functionality, dependencies, and interfaces to determine the subset of test cases that need to be re-executed. Testers analyze the change request or user story, review associated requirements, and identify the functionalities or components likely affected by the change. By conducting impact analysis using tools like SonarQube or Dependency-Check, testers can prioritize test cases that cover the impacted areas and verify the correctness and integrity of the software after the change.

bashCopy code

```
sonar-scanner
```

This command invokes the SonarQube scanner tool to perform static code analysis and assess the impact of code changes on software quality and maintainability, providing insights into potential areas requiring regression testing.

Risk-Based Selection: Risk-based regression test selection techniques prioritize test cases based on the perceived risk or potential impact of software changes on critical business functions, user experience, and system stability. Testers assess the risk associated with each change using risk analysis techniques like Failure Mode and Effects

Analysis (FMEA) or Risk Priority Number (RPN) calculation. By assigning risk levels to individual test cases and focusing regression testing efforts on high-risk areas, testers can mitigate the likelihood of regression defects and prioritize testing activities effectively.

bashCopy code

```
fmea analyze --input <requirements.csv> --output <risk-assessment.xlsx>
```

This command performs Failure Mode and Effects Analysis (FMEA) on the requirements specified in a CSV file (<requirements.csv>) and generates a risk assessment report in Excel format (<risk-assessment.xlsx>), helping testers identify high-risk areas for regression testing.

Traceability-Based Selection: Traceability-based regression test selection techniques establish traceability links between requirements, test cases, and source code to facilitate impact analysis and test prioritization. Testers map each test case to the corresponding requirements or user stories and trace changes in requirements to related test cases. By leveraging traceability matrices or tools like Jira or IBM Rational DOORS, testers can identify the test cases affected by specific requirements changes and selectively re-execute them to validate the correctness and completeness of the software.

bashCopy code

```
jira search 'issueType = Requirement AND affectedVersion = "1.0"'
```

This command searches for requirements in Jira that are associated with a specific software version ("1.0"), enabling testers to identify the requirements impacted by version changes and determine the corresponding test cases for regression testing.

Model-Based Selection: Model-based regression test selection techniques use mathematical models, such as finite state machines or state transition diagrams, to represent the behavior and interactions of software components. Testers derive test cases from these models and prioritize them based on model coverage and transition coverage criteria. By simulating software behavior using model-based testing tools like Spec Explorer or GraphWalker, testers can identify the critical paths, states, and transitions affected by software changes and focus regression testing efforts on validating these areas.

bashCopy code

```
specexplorer generate-tests --model <model.xml> --coverage transition --output <test-cases.xml>
```

This command generates test cases from a specified model file (<model.xml>) using Spec Explorer and prioritizes them based on transition coverage criteria, producing an XML file containing the generated test cases (<test-cases.xml>) for regression testing.

Historical Data-Based Selection: Historical data-based regression test selection techniques leverage past testing results, defect reports, and code change history to identify recurring patterns, areas of frequent defects, and regression-prone modules. Testers analyze historical test execution data, defect trends, and code churn metrics to prioritize test cases for regression testing. By focusing on historically problematic areas and frequently changed modules, testers can allocate testing resources more effectively and mitigate the risk of regression defects in those areas.

bashCopy code

```
git log --author=<developer> --since=<date> --oneline
```
This command retrieves the commit history of a specific developer (<developer>) since a specified date (<date>) from a Git repository, helping testers analyze the developer's contribution to code changes and identify modules requiring regression testing.

By employing regression test selection techniques tailored to the specific context, complexity, and risk profile of the software under test, organizations can optimize testing efforts, reduce testing cycle time, and ensure the stability and reliability of software releases. Effective regression test selection enables testers to strike a balance between test coverage and resource constraints, facilitating faster time-to-market and enhancing overall software quality and customer satisfaction.

Chapter 6: Performance Testing Essentials

Performance testing fundamentals are essential aspects of software testing that focus on evaluating the speed, responsiveness, stability, and scalability of software applications under various workload conditions to ensure optimal performance and user experience. Performance testing encompasses a range of techniques, methodologies, and tools aimed at identifying performance bottlenecks, optimizing system resources, and mitigating risks associated with performance degradation or failure in production environments. By conducting performance testing, organizations can proactively address performance-related issues, enhance system reliability, and deliver high-quality software that meets user expectations and business requirements.

Performance testing involves evaluating different aspects of software performance, including response time, throughput, resource utilization, and concurrency, to assess how well the software performs under normal and peak load conditions. Various types of performance testing, such as load testing, stress testing, and scalability testing, help testers simulate real-world usage scenarios and identify performance constraints and limitations that could impact user satisfaction and business operations.

Load Testing: Load testing is a fundamental performance testing technique that involves assessing the software's behavior and performance under expected load conditions to determine its reliability and scalability. Load testing simulates multiple concurrent users or transactions to measure the system's response time, throughput, and resource utilization under typical usage scenarios. By gradually increasing the load on the system, testers can identify performance bottlenecks, such as slow response times or resource exhaustion, and optimize system configurations to improve performance and stability.

To conduct load testing using a tool like Apache JMeter, testers can create a test plan that defines the desired load scenario, configure the number of virtual users, and specify the target system endpoints. They can then execute the test plan using the CLI command:

bashCopy code

```
jmeter -n -t testplan.jmx -l results.csv
```

This command runs JMeter in non-GUI mode ("-n") with the specified test plan file ("testplan.jmx") and saves the test results to a CSV file ("results.csv") for analysis.

Stress Testing: Stress testing evaluates the software's stability and robustness by subjecting it to extreme load conditions beyond its normal operational capacity to identify failure points and determine the system's breaking point. Stress testing simulates scenarios such as sudden spikes in user traffic, database overload, or resource exhaustion to assess how well the system handles stress and recovers from failures. By pushing the system to its limits, testers can uncover performance issues, such as memory leaks or database deadlocks, and implement measures to enhance system resilience and fault tolerance.

To perform stress testing using tools like Apache JMeter, testers can create a stress test plan that includes aggressive load profiles and scenarios designed to stress system resources. They can execute the stress test plan using the CLI command:

bashCopy code

jmeter -n -t stress-test-plan.jmx -l stress-test-results.csv

This command runs JMeter in non-GUI mode with the specified stress test plan file and saves the stress test results to a CSV file for analysis.

Scalability Testing: Scalability testing evaluates the software's ability to handle increasing workload volumes and user loads while maintaining performance, responsiveness, and stability. Scalability testing aims to assess how well the system scales horizontally or vertically to accommodate growing user demands and data volumes without compromising performance or reliability. By measuring key performance indicators such as response time, throughput, and resource utilization under varying load levels, testers can determine the system's scalability limits and scalability factors and optimize system architecture and configurations accordingly.

To conduct scalability testing using tools like Apache JMeter, testers can design test scenarios that simulate incremental load increases over time or sudden bursts of user activity. They can execute the scalability test scenarios using the CLI command:

bashCopy code

jmeter -n -t scalability-test-plan.jmx -l scalability-test-results.csv

This command runs JMeter in non-GUI mode with the specified scalability test plan file and saves the scalability test results to a CSV file for analysis.

Endurance Testing: Endurance testing, also known as soak testing or longevity testing, evaluates the software's stability and performance over an extended period under sustained load conditions to assess its reliability and robustness over time. Endurance testing aims to identify memory leaks, resource leaks, or performance degradation issues that may occur during prolonged usage or continuous operation. By monitoring system metrics such as memory usage, CPU utilization, and database connections, testers can detect performance anomalies or degradation trends and take preventive actions to maintain system integrity and availability.

To perform endurance testing using tools like Apache JMeter, testers can design test scenarios that simulate continuous user activity or steady-state workloads over an extended duration. They can execute the endurance test scenarios using the CLI command:

bashCopy code

```
jmeter -n -t endurance-test-plan.jmx -l endurance-test-results.csv
```

This command runs JMeter in non-GUI mode with the specified endurance test plan file and saves the endurance test results to a CSV file for analysis.

Performance testing fundamentals play a critical role in ensuring the reliability, scalability, and responsiveness of software applications in real-world environments. By applying performance testing techniques effectively and leveraging performance testing tools and methodologies, organizations can optimize system performance, enhance user satisfaction, and achieve their business objectives effectively.

Performance metrics and analysis play a pivotal role in evaluating the efficiency, responsiveness, and scalability of software applications, providing insights into system behavior and identifying opportunities for optimization and improvement. Performance testing generates a wealth of metrics that measure various aspects of application performance, including response times, throughput, resource utilization, and error rates, enabling stakeholders to assess performance bottlenecks, validate performance requirements, and make informed decisions about performance tuning and capacity planning. By analyzing performance metrics, organizations can identify trends, patterns, and anomalies in application performance, diagnose performance issues, and prioritize optimization efforts to enhance user experience and maximize system efficiency.

Response Time: Response time is one of the fundamental performance metrics that measures the time taken for the system to respond to user requests or transactions. It includes the time elapsed between sending a request to the system and receiving a corresponding response, encompassing network latency, server processing time, and client rendering time. Response time metrics help assess system responsiveness and identify performance bottlenecks that contribute to delays in request processing.

To measure response time using a command-line tool like Apache JMeter, testers can configure HTTP Request samplers to simulate user interactions with the application and record response times for each request. For example, the following JMeter command executes a test plan named "performance-test.jmx" and generates a summary report with response time metrics:
bashCopy code

```
jmeter -n -t performance-test.jmx -l test-results.jtl -e -o
report-directory
```

Throughput: Throughput measures the rate at which the system processes transactions or requests over a specified period, indicating the system's capacity to handle concurrent user load. It represents the volume of data or transactions processed per unit of time and is often expressed in requests per second (RPS) or transactions per minute (TPM). Throughput metrics help assess system scalability and capacity under varying load conditions.

To measure throughput using JMeter, testers can analyze the transaction throughput metric reported in test results. JMeter provides aggregate throughput statistics in the generated test report, indicating the average number of transactions processed per second during the test execution. Testers can use this metric to assess the system's capacity to handle user load and identify performance constraints.

Error Rate: Error rate measures the frequency of errors or failures encountered during performance testing, including HTTP errors, timeouts, and connection failures. It quantifies the reliability and robustness of the system under load and helps identify defects, vulnerabilities, and performance bottlenecks that contribute to error-prone behavior. Monitoring error rates enables testers to diagnose and prioritize resolution of critical issues impacting system stability and user experience.

To monitor error rates using JMeter, testers can configure listeners such as the Summary Report or Aggregate Report to display error count and percentage metrics for each sampler or transaction. By analyzing error rate trends over time and correlating them with system metrics, testers can pinpoint performance issues and assess their impact on overall system health.

Resource Utilization: Resource utilization metrics quantify the consumption of system resources, such as CPU, memory, disk I/O, and network bandwidth, during performance testing. They provide insights into resource contention, saturation, and inefficiencies that affect application performance and scalability. Monitoring resource utilization helps identify resource-intensive components, optimize resource allocation, and ensure efficient resource management to support desired levels of performance.

To measure resource utilization using command-line tools like SAR (System Activity Reporter) on Linux systems, testers can run the following command to collect CPU utilization metrics at regular intervals:

bashCopy code

```
sar -u 1 10
```

This command collects CPU utilization data every second for a duration of 10 seconds and displays statistics such as user CPU time, system CPU time, and idle CPU time. Testers can analyze CPU utilization trends and identify periods of high CPU usage that may impact application performance.

Concurrency and Scalability: Concurrency and scalability metrics evaluate the system's ability to handle simultaneous user interactions and scale resources to accommodate increasing workload demands. They measure factors such as concurrent user sessions, transaction throughput under load, and system response times as the user load increases. Concurrency and scalability testing help assess system performance under varying load conditions and validate its ability to support anticipated user growth and workload fluctuations.

To analyze concurrency and scalability using JMeter, testers can configure Thread Group settings to simulate a specified number of concurrent users or threads accessing the application concurrently. By gradually increasing the thread count and monitoring performance metrics, testers can identify performance bottlenecks, evaluate system scalability, and determine the maximum sustainable user load.

Latency and Network Performance: Latency and network performance metrics assess the time taken for data packets to travel between client and server components, measuring network latency, round-trip time, and data transmission speeds. They help evaluate the efficiency and reliability of network communication, identify network bottlenecks, and optimize network configurations to minimize latency and improve data transfer rates.

To measure latency and network performance using tools like Wireshark, testers can capture network traffic between client and server components and analyze packet timestamps, sequence numbers, and round-trip times. Wireshark provides detailed packet-level insights into network behavior, allowing testers to identify latency issues, packet loss, and network congestion that may impact application performance.

User Experience Metrics: User experience metrics evaluate subjective aspects of application performance, including perceived responsiveness, usability, and satisfaction from end-user perspectives. They encompass metrics such as page load times, transaction completion rates, and user feedback ratings collected through surveys or feedback forms. User experience metrics provide valuable insights into user perception of application performance and help prioritize optimization efforts to enhance user satisfaction and retention.

To collect user experience metrics, testers can integrate real user monitoring (RUM) tools or application performance monitoring (APM) solutions into the application infrastructure to capture user interactions, page load times, and session durations in real time. These tools provide dashboards and reports displaying user experience metrics, allowing testers to monitor performance trends, identify user pain points, and prioritize enhancements to improve overall user satisfaction.

By leveraging performance metrics and analysis techniques, organizations can gain a comprehensive understanding of application performance, diagnose performance issues, and optimize system behavior to meet user expectations and business objectives. Performance testing serves as a cornerstone of software quality assurance, ensuring that applications deliver the required performance, reliability, and scalability to support business-critical operations and deliver exceptional user experiences.

Chapter 7: Load and Stress Testing Strategies

Load testing forms a fundamental aspect of performance testing, focusing on evaluating the behavior and performance of a software application under specific load conditions. Load testing involves subjecting the application to simulated user loads, mimicking real-world usage scenarios to assess its ability to handle concurrent user interactions, process transactions, and sustain performance levels under varying levels of workload. Load testing helps identify performance bottlenecks, scalability issues, and resource constraints that may impact application performance and user experience, enabling organizations to optimize system configurations, enhance scalability, and ensure reliable performance under production conditions.

Understanding Load Testing Concepts: Load testing simulates user activity by generating virtual users or client requests to interact with the application, measuring system response times, throughput, and resource utilization under load. Test scenarios are designed to replicate anticipated user behaviors, such as browsing web pages, submitting forms, or performing transactions, to assess application performance under typical usage patterns. Load testing evaluates system behavior at different load levels, ranging from moderate to peak loads, to validate performance scalability and identify performance limits.

To initiate a basic load test using Apache JMeter, testers can create a test plan that includes HTTP Request samplers to simulate user interactions and configure Thread Group settings to define the number of concurrent users or threads. The following command executes a JMeter test plan named "load-test.jmx" in non-GUI mode with 100 concurrent users for a duration of 5 minutes: bashCopy code

```
jmeter -n -t load-test.jmx -l test-results.jtl -e -o report-directory -Jusers=100 -Jduration=300
```

Defining Load Test Scenarios: Load test scenarios are designed based on anticipated user behavior, application usage patterns, and performance objectives. Testers identify critical user journeys, transactions, or workflows within the application and create test scripts or scenarios to simulate these interactions under load. Load test scenarios may include activities such as logging in, searching for products, adding items to a shopping cart, or processing checkout transactions, representing typical user interactions and business processes.

To create load test scenarios using JMeter, testers can define HTTP Request samplers to simulate user actions, parameterize test data to emulate dynamic user inputs, and configure test logic using controllers and conditional elements. By designing realistic load test scenarios, testers can replicate actual user behavior and workload patterns to evaluate application performance accurately.

Setting Load Test Goals and Metrics: Load testing establishes specific performance goals and metrics to measure and evaluate application performance under load. Testers define key performance indicators (KPIs) such as response times, throughput, error rates, and resource utilization thresholds to assess system performance against predefined benchmarks or service

131

level agreements (SLAs). Load test goals help align testing objectives with business requirements and ensure that application performance meets user expectations and performance targets.

To set load test goals and metrics, testers can define performance acceptance criteria and thresholds for each performance metric based on business requirements and user expectations. Load test scripts can include assertions and validation checks to verify that performance metrics meet predefined criteria during test execution. By monitoring and analyzing performance metrics, testers can assess system performance, identify performance bottlenecks, and measure compliance with performance objectives.

Creating Load Profiles: Load testing involves creating load profiles that define the distribution and intensity of user load over time. Load profiles specify parameters such as the number of concurrent users, transaction rates, and ramp-up and ramp-down periods to simulate realistic user behavior and workload patterns. Testers design load profiles based on usage statistics, traffic patterns, and peak load projections to validate application performance under varying load conditions.

To create load profiles in JMeter, testers can configure Thread Group settings to specify the number of threads (users) and define ramp-up and ramp-down periods to simulate gradual increases and decreases in user load over time. Testers can also use timers and pacing controllers to control the rate of user requests and distribute load evenly across test scenarios. By defining load profiles, testers can replicate real-world usage scenarios and evaluate application performance across different load levels.

Executing Load Tests: Load tests are executed by running load test scenarios against the application under test to generate user load and measure system performance metrics. Testers execute load tests using dedicated load testing tools or frameworks that simulate user interactions, monitor system behavior, and collect performance data in real time. Load test execution involves configuring test parameters, running test scenarios, monitoring system metrics, and analyzing test results to assess application performance under load.

To execute a load test using JMeter, testers can run the JMeter command-line interface (CLI) with the specified test plan and configuration parameters. JMeter generates user load, sends requests to the application server, measures response times, and collects performance metrics during test execution. Testers monitor test progress and analyze test results to identify performance issues, bottlenecks, and areas for optimization.

Analyzing Load Test Results: Load test results provide valuable insights into application performance, highlighting performance bottlenecks, scalability limitations, and areas for optimization. Testers analyze load test results to identify performance trends, anomalies, and deviations from expected behavior, correlating performance metrics with system behavior and resource utilization data. Load test analysis involves comparing performance metrics against predefined thresholds, identifying root causes of performance issues, and prioritizing remediation efforts.

To analyze load test results using JMeter, testers can generate comprehensive test reports and performance dashboards that visualize performance metrics, trends, and distribution statistics. JMeter provides built-in listeners and reporting tools to generate HTML, CSV, or XML reports containing performance data, charts, and graphs. Testers analyze load test reports to identify performance bottlenecks, assess system scalability, and validate compliance with performance objectives.

By mastering the basics of load testing and applying best practices in load test design, execution, and analysis, organizations can ensure that their applications deliver optimal performance, scalability, and reliability under varying workload conditions. Load testing serves as a critical component of software quality assurance, enabling organizations to proactively identify and address performance issues, optimize system performance, and deliver exceptional user experiences.

Stress testing forms an integral part of performance testing, focusing on evaluating the robustness, stability, and resilience of software applications under extreme or beyond-normal load conditions. Unlike load testing, which assesses application performance under expected user loads, stress testing subjects the application to excessive loads, resource exhaustion, and adverse conditions to identify its breaking points, failure modes, and capacity limits. Stress testing helps uncover vulnerabilities, memory leaks, concurrency issues, and performance bottlenecks that may lead to system instability, crashes, or degradation under stress. By simulating extreme load scenarios and monitoring application behavior, stress testing enables organizations to validate system reliability, enhance fault tolerance, and improve overall system resilience to withstand peak loads and adverse conditions.

Understanding Stress Testing Objectives: Stress testing aims to assess the application's behavior under extreme conditions, such as high user loads, excessive data volumes, or resource constraints, to identify performance degradation, system failures, and scalability limitations. The primary objectives of stress testing include determining the application's breaking points, evaluating its ability to recover from failures, and assessing its resilience and stability under stress. Stress testing helps organizations identify critical performance bottlenecks, vulnerabilities, and weaknesses that may impact application reliability and user experience under adverse conditions.

To initiate stress testing using Apache JMeter, testers can design test scenarios that simulate extreme load conditions and configure test scripts to generate excessive user traffic, spike loads, or resource-intensive operations. By specifying high load levels and aggressive pacing, testers can stress the application to assess its performance under extreme conditions and identify potential failure points.

Defining Stress Test Scenarios: Stress test scenarios are designed to simulate extreme load conditions, adverse events, and worst-case scenarios that may impact application performance and stability. Testers identify stress factors, such as high user concurrency, rapid transaction rates, or resource contention, and create test scripts or scenarios to replicate these conditions during stress testing. Stress test scenarios may include activities such as generating concurrent user sessions, saturating system resources, or overwhelming backend services to assess application behavior under extreme load conditions.

To define stress test scenarios using JMeter, testers can configure Thread Group settings to specify high thread counts, short ramp-up times, and continuous load generation to simulate stress conditions. Test scripts may include resource-intensive operations, database queries, or API calls that exert pressure on the application and stress its performance capabilities. By designing realistic stress test scenarios, testers can evaluate the application's resilience and robustness under extreme load conditions and identify potential failure points.

Creating Stress Test Workloads: Stress test workloads represent the distribution and intensity of user load or activity during stress testing, determining the magnitude and impact of stress conditions on application performance. Testers create stress test workloads by defining parameters such as the number of concurrent users, transaction rates, think times, and data volumes to simulate realistic stress scenarios. Stress test workloads may include bursty traffic patterns, uneven user distributions, or random spikes in load to assess the application's response to unpredictable and fluctuating workload conditions.

To create stress test workloads using JMeter, testers can configure Thread Group settings to specify thread counts, ramp-up periods, and loop counts that generate high user concurrency and transaction rates. Additionally, testers can use timers and pacing controllers to introduce variability and randomness into the workload, simulating real-world user behavior and load patterns. By defining diverse and dynamic stress test workloads, testers can assess the application's performance resilience and responsiveness under varying stress conditions.

Simulating Stress Conditions: Stress testing simulates stress conditions by generating extreme load levels, resource constraints, or adverse events to evaluate application behavior under challenging circumstances. Testers use stress testing tools or frameworks to simulate stress conditions, such as CPU spikes, memory leaks, network failures, or database overload, to assess the application's response and resilience under stress. Stress testing may involve gradually increasing load levels, introducing sudden load spikes, or imposing resource constraints to identify system breaking points and failure modes.

To simulate stress conditions using JMeter, testers can configure test scripts to generate high user loads, aggressive pacing, and resource-intensive operations that stress the application components. By gradually increasing the load levels or introducing random spikes in load, testers can assess the application's ability to handle peak loads and recover from performance degradation. Stress testing tools provide features to monitor system metrics, detect errors, and capture performance data during stress testing to identify system weaknesses and areas for improvement.

Monitoring and Analyzing Stress Test Results: Stress test results provide insights into application behavior under extreme load conditions, highlighting performance degradation, system failures, and scalability limitations. Testers monitor stress test results in real time and analyze performance metrics, error logs, and system behavior to identify critical issues, bottlenecks, and failure points. Stress test analysis involves correlating performance metrics with stress conditions, identifying root causes of performance degradation, and prioritizing remediation efforts to improve system resilience and stability.

To monitor stress test results using JMeter, testers can use built-in listeners and reporting tools to visualize performance metrics, errors, and response times during stress testing. JMeter provides graphical reports, charts, and graphs that display performance trends, distribution statistics, and error rates, allowing testers to identify performance anomalies and areas for optimization. By analyzing stress test results, testers can assess application reliability, resilience, and scalability under extreme load conditions and implement corrective measures to enhance system performance and stability.

By employing stress testing approaches and best practices, organizations can validate application reliability, resilience, and stability under extreme load conditions, mitigate performance risks, and ensure optimal user experience and satisfaction. Stress testing serves as a critical component of performance testing, enabling organizations to identify and address performance bottlenecks, scalability limitations, and system weaknesses before deployment to production environments.

Chapter 8: Integration Testing Principles

Integration testing plays a crucial role in software development, focusing on validating the interactions and interfaces between individual software components to ensure they function correctly together as a cohesive system. Unlike unit testing, which verifies the correctness of individual modules or components in isolation, integration testing evaluates the integration points, data flows, and dependencies between interconnected modules, subsystems, or services. Integration testing helps detect defects, interoperability issues, and integration failures early in the development lifecycle, facilitating early bug detection, defect resolution, and system stabilization. By verifying the integration of software components and validating end-to-end system behavior, integration testing mitigates integration risks, enhances software quality, and ensures the reliability and consistency of complex software systems.

Understanding Integration Testing Concepts: Integration testing verifies the interaction and collaboration between software components, validating the flow of data, control, and communication across interconnected modules, services, or layers of the application architecture. Integration testing exercises integrated software units, subsystems, or interfaces to validate their functionality, interoperability, and compatibility with other components in the system. Unlike unit testing, which isolates individual components, integration testing evaluates the behavior of integrated components in conjunction, detecting integration defects, interface mismatches, and communication errors that may impact system functionality and performance.

To perform integration testing using Apache Maven, testers can configure Maven build scripts to execute integration tests alongside unit tests, integrating multiple modules or components into a single test suite. Maven provides plugins such as the Maven Surefire Plugin and Maven Failsafe Plugin for running unit tests and integration tests respectively. By defining integration test dependencies and configuring test execution parameters, testers can automate the execution of integration tests as part of the software build process, ensuring comprehensive test coverage and early detection of integration issues.

Types of Integration Testing: Integration testing encompasses various testing approaches and techniques, including top-down integration testing, bottom-up integration testing, and hybrid integration testing strategies. Top-down integration testing begins with the testing of higher-level modules or subsystems, progressively integrating lower-level modules until the entire system is tested as a whole. Conversely, bottom-up integration testing starts with testing lower-level modules or units, gradually integrating higher-level modules until the entire system is validated. Hybrid integration testing combines elements of both top-down and bottom-up approaches, leveraging stubs, drivers, or mock objects to simulate missing or unavailable components during testing.

To implement integration testing strategies using JUnit, testers can create test classes and methods to verify the interactions between integrated components or modules. JUnit provides annotations such as @Before, @After, and @Test for defining setup, teardown, and test methods respectively. Testers can use mocking frameworks such as Mockito or EasyMock to simulate dependencies or external services during integration testing, isolating components for testing and validating their interactions in controlled environments. By adopting different integration testing techniques, testers can verify system behavior, identify integration issues, and ensure the compatibility and consistency of integrated components.

Integration Testing Approaches: Integration testing can be performed using various approaches, including component integration testing, system integration testing, and interface integration testing. Component integration testing focuses on verifying the interactions and integration of individual software components or modules within a subsystem or layer of the application architecture. System integration testing validates the integration and interoperability of multiple subsystems or modules within the entire software system, ensuring that the system functions as intended when all components are integrated together. Interface integration testing verifies the communication and data exchange between interconnected systems, services, or external interfaces, validating the compatibility and correctness of interface interactions.

To execute component integration tests using Gradle, testers can define integration test tasks and configurations in the Gradle build scripts to compile, package, and deploy integrated components for testing. Gradle provides plugins such as the Gradle Test Plugin and

Gradle Integration Testing Plugin for running unit tests and integration tests respectively. Testers can configure test environments, dependencies, and test resources for integration testing using Gradle, ensuring that integrated components are tested in isolation and in conjunction with other modules or subsystems. By adopting integration testing approaches, testers can validate system integration, detect integration defects, and ensure the reliability and consistency of integrated software systems.

Challenges in Integration Testing: Integration testing poses several challenges, including test environment setup, test data management, dependency management, and test orchestration. Establishing test environments that accurately replicate production configurations and dependencies can be complex and time-consuming, requiring careful configuration and provisioning of test resources, databases, and external services. Managing test data for integration testing, including generating realistic test data sets, ensuring data consistency, and maintaining data privacy and security, presents additional challenges for testers. Dependency management involves handling dependencies between integrated components, libraries, frameworks, and external services, ensuring compatibility, versioning, and configuration consistency across the integrated system. Test orchestration involves coordinating the execution of integration tests, managing test suites, dependencies, and execution sequences, and aggregating test results for analysis and reporting.

To address challenges in integration testing, testers can use containerization technologies such as Docker or Kubernetes to create isolated test environments, containerize dependencies, and orchestrate test execution across distributed environments. Docker provides commands such as docker build, docker run, and docker-compose for building, running, and orchestrating containerized test environments. Testers can use Docker images to package dependencies, configurations, and test scripts, ensuring consistent and reproducible test environments across different development, testing, and production environments. By leveraging containerization and orchestration tools, testers can streamline test environment setup, dependency management, and test execution, accelerating the integration testing process and improving test efficiency and reliability.

By understanding integration testing concepts, adopting integration testing approaches, and addressing challenges in integration testing, organizations can validate system integration, detect integration defects, and ensure the reliability and consistency of integrated software systems. Integration testing serves as a critical component of the software testing lifecycle, enabling organizations to verify the interoperability, compatibility, and functionality of integrated components, subsystems, and interfaces, and deliver high-quality software products to end-users.

Integration testing strategies encompass various approaches and methodologies aimed at validating the interaction and interoperability of software components, subsystems, or modules within a larger system or application architecture. These strategies play a crucial role in ensuring the seamless integration of individual components and the overall functionality, reliability, and performance of the system. Integration testing verifies the behavior of integrated components, data flows, and communication protocols to identify integration defects, interoperability issues, and interface inconsistencies early in the development lifecycle, enabling timely resolution and system stabilization. By adopting effective integration testing strategies, organizations can enhance software quality, mitigate integration risks, and deliver robust and reliable software solutions to end-users.

Top-Down Integration Testing: Top-down integration testing is a progressive testing approach that begins with testing higher-level modules or subsystems before integrating lower-level modules or components. In this approach, testing progresses downward through the application hierarchy, with higher-level modules serving as the entry point for integration testing. Stub or mock implementations may be used to simulate the behavior of lower-level modules or components that are not yet available. Top-down integration testing focuses on verifying the interactions and interfaces between integrated modules, validating system behavior from a high-level perspective, and ensuring that higher-level functionality is not compromised by integration issues.

To implement top-down integration testing using JUnit, testers can create test classes and methods to verify the behavior of higher-level modules or subsystems, mocking or stubbing dependencies on lower-level components or services. JUnit provides annotations such as @RunWith and @Mock for integrating mocking frameworks such as Mockito or EasyMock into test cases. Testers can simulate the behavior of lower-level modules by defining mock objects or stubs that mimic the expected behavior of dependencies, allowing for isolated testing of higher-level functionality. By adopting top-down integration testing, testers can identify integration issues early in the development lifecycle, validate system behavior from a user perspective, and ensure the integrity and correctness of higher-level functionality.

Bottom-Up Integration Testing: Bottom-up integration testing is a complementary approach to top-down integration testing, focusing on testing lower-level modules or components before integrating higher-level modules or subsystems. In this approach, testing progresses upward through the application hierarchy, with lower-level modules serving as the foundation for integration testing. Drivers or harnesses may be used to simulate the behavior of higher-level modules or components that are not yet available. Bottom-up integration testing validates the functionality and interfaces of integrated components from a low-level perspective, ensuring that individual modules behave as expected and can interact seamlessly with higher-level modules.

To perform bottom-up integration testing using Apache Maven, testers can configure Maven build scripts to compile, package, and deploy lower-level modules or components for integration testing. Maven provides plugins such as the Maven Compiler Plugin and Maven Jar Plugin for compiling Java source code and creating JAR files respectively. Testers can define test dependencies and configure test execution parameters in Maven's pom.xml file to execute integration tests for lower-level modules or components. By automating the build and testing process using Maven, testers can streamline bottom-up integration testing, validate the functionality of individual modules, and identify integration issues early in the development lifecycle.

Hybrid Integration Testing: Hybrid integration testing combines elements of both top-down and bottom-up integration testing approaches, leveraging the strengths of each approach to validate system integration comprehensively. In hybrid integration testing, testing progresses iteratively through the application hierarchy, with a mix of top-down and bottom-up testing strategies employed based on the availability and maturity of integrated components. Stubbing, mocking, or simulating dependencies may be used to isolate components for testing and to facilitate integration testing in stages. Hybrid integration testing aims to balance the advantages of both top-down and bottom-up approaches, enabling comprehensive validation of system integration while maximizing testing efficiency and effectiveness.

To implement hybrid integration testing using Gradle, testers can define integration test tasks and configurations in the Gradle build scripts to execute both top-down and bottom-up integration tests as part of the software build process. Gradle provides plugins such as the Gradle Test Plugin and Gradle Integration Testing Plugin for running unit tests and integration tests respectively. Testers can configure test environments, dependencies, and test resources for hybrid integration testing using Gradle, ensuring that integrated components are tested in isolation and in conjunction with other modules or subsystems. By adopting hybrid integration testing, testers can validate system integration from multiple perspectives, identify integration issues comprehensively, and ensure the reliability and consistency of integrated software systems.

Integration testing strategies are essential for verifying the interaction and interoperability of software components, subsystems, or modules within complex software systems. By adopting top-down, bottom-up, or hybrid integration testing approaches, organizations can validate system integration, detect integration defects, and ensure the reliability and consistency of integrated software solutions. Integration testing plays a critical role in the software development lifecycle, enabling organizations to deliver high-quality software products that meet the expectations and requirements of end-users.

Chapter 9: Acceptance Testing Best Practices

Acceptance testing, a pivotal phase in the software development lifecycle, involves evaluating a software system's compliance with business requirements and ensuring that it meets the needs of end-users. Unlike other testing phases that focus on technical aspects, acceptance testing centers on verifying the software's functionality, usability, and suitability for real-world scenarios. Acceptance testing encompasses various techniques and methodologies aimed at validating the software's adherence to user expectations, business objectives, and regulatory standards. This testing phase serves as a bridge between development and deployment, facilitating collaboration between stakeholders, developers, and testers to ensure the delivery of high-quality software products that align with user needs and organizational goals.

Understanding Acceptance Testing Concepts: Acceptance testing validates whether a software system meets predefined acceptance criteria and satisfies the needs of stakeholders and end-users. It assesses the software's functionality, usability, reliability, and performance in real-world scenarios, ensuring that it delivers value and meets business objectives. Acceptance testing may involve different stakeholders, including business analysts, product owners, customers, and end-users, who collaborate to define acceptance criteria, user stories, and test scenarios. This testing phase focuses on validating user requirements, verifying business logic, and ensuring that the software meets regulatory compliance and industry standards.

To initiate acceptance testing using Selenium WebDriver, testers can write automated test scripts using programming languages such as Java, Python, or C#. Selenium WebDriver provides a set of APIs for interacting with web elements, performing actions, and validating results. Testers can use commands such as findElement, click, sendKeys, and assert to interact with web elements, simulate user actions, and verify expected outcomes. By automating acceptance tests with Selenium WebDriver, testers can validate web applications against acceptance criteria, streamline test execution, and accelerate the delivery of high-quality software products.

Types of Acceptance Testing: Acceptance testing encompasses various types, including user acceptance testing (UAT), alpha testing, beta testing, and regulatory acceptance testing. User acceptance testing involves end-users or business stakeholders validating the software's functionality, usability, and suitability for their needs. Alpha testing is conducted internally by the development team to identify defects and issues before releasing the software to external users. Beta testing involves releasing the software to a limited group of external users or customers to gather feedback and identify issues in real-world environments. Regulatory acceptance testing verifies that the software complies with industry regulations, standards, and legal requirements.

To perform user acceptance testing using JIRA, testers can create user stories, acceptance criteria, and test scenarios as JIRA issues or epics. JIRA provides features for organizing and prioritizing user stories, defining acceptance criteria, and tracking testing progress. Testers can use JIRA workflows to transition issues through different states, such as "To Do," "In Progress," "In Review," and "Done." By using JIRA boards and dashboards, testers can visualize testing progress, identify bottlenecks, and collaborate with stakeholders to ensure that user acceptance testing is conducted effectively and efficiently.

Automated Acceptance Testing: Automated acceptance testing involves using automated test scripts and tools to validate software functionality, user interactions, and business processes. Automation helps accelerate testing cycles, improve test coverage, and detect defects early in the development lifecycle. Automated acceptance tests can be executed repeatedly, ensuring consistent validation of software functionality across different environments and configurations. Test automation frameworks such as Cucumber, SpecFlow, and Robot Framework facilitate the creation and execution of automated acceptance tests, enabling testers to write tests in natural language format and collaborate with non-technical stakeholders.

Acceptance criteria definition is a critical aspect of the software development process, outlining specific conditions and requirements that must be met for a product or feature to be considered acceptable to stakeholders. These criteria serve as measurable standards against which the functionality and quality of the software are evaluated, ensuring alignment with business objectives and user expectations. Effective acceptance criteria are clear, concise, and unambiguous, providing guidance to developers, testers, and stakeholders throughout the development lifecycle. By defining acceptance criteria early in the project, teams can ensure that everyone understands the expectations for the deliverables and can work towards meeting those expectations efficiently.

Understanding Acceptance Criteria: Acceptance criteria are a set of conditions or specifications that define the functionality, behavior, and performance expectations for a software product or feature. They articulate the "what" rather than the "how" of a requirement, focusing on the desired outcomes rather than implementation details. Acceptance criteria are typically written from the perspective of end-users or stakeholders, describing the functionality or behavior they expect to see in the final product. These criteria may include functional requirements, user interface specifications, performance benchmarks, and regulatory compliance standards.

To define acceptance criteria using Agile methodologies, teams can leverage user stories as a framework for capturing requirements and expectations. User stories follow a specific template that includes a description of the desired functionality, acceptance criteria, and priority level. For example, a user story for an e-commerce website may state, "As a customer, I want to be able to add items to my shopping cart, so that I can purchase them later." Acceptance criteria for this user story could include requirements such as the ability to add items to the cart, update quantities, and view the total price before checkout.

Characteristics of Effective Acceptance Criteria: Effective acceptance criteria exhibit several key characteristics that make them valuable for guiding the development process. Firstly, acceptance criteria should be specific and measurable, providing clear guidelines for what constitutes successful implementation. They should also be achievable and realistic, reflecting the capabilities and constraints of the development team and technology stack. Additionally, acceptance criteria should be relevant to the business objectives and user needs, ensuring that the delivered product adds value and meets customer expectations.

To create effective acceptance criteria, teams can use the SMART criteria framework, which stands for Specific, Measurable, Achievable, Relevant, and Time-bound. By applying these principles, teams can ensure that acceptance criteria are well-defined, quantifiable, feasible, aligned with business goals, and time-bound to project milestones. For example, a SMART acceptance criterion for a software feature might state, "The login page must load in under two seconds, allowing users to access their accounts quickly and efficiently."

Collaborative Definition of Acceptance Criteria: The process of defining acceptance criteria is inherently collaborative, involving input from various stakeholders, including product owners, business analysts, developers, and testers. Collaborative definition ensures that all perspectives and requirements are considered, resulting in comprehensive and accurate acceptance criteria. Stakeholders contribute their domain expertise, business knowledge, and user insights to ensure that acceptance criteria reflect the needs and priorities of end-users and the organization.

To facilitate collaborative definition of acceptance criteria, teams can use techniques such as workshops, brainstorming sessions, and user story mapping exercises. These activities bring together stakeholders from different departments and roles to discuss requirements, clarify expectations, and align on acceptance criteria. During these sessions, teams can use visual aids such as whiteboards, sticky notes, and diagrams to capture ideas, prioritize features, and define acceptance criteria collaboratively. By involving stakeholders throughout the acceptance criteria definition process, teams can foster a shared understanding of project goals and requirements, leading to better outcomes and increased stakeholder satisfaction.

Validation and Iteration of Acceptance Criteria: Once acceptance criteria are defined, they undergo validation and iteration to ensure their accuracy, completeness, and relevance. Validation involves reviewing acceptance criteria against business requirements, user needs, and project constraints to verify their alignment and suitability. Iteration involves refining and updating acceptance criteria based on feedback, changes in project scope, or evolving business priorities. Validation and iteration are ongoing processes that occur throughout the development lifecycle, ensuring that acceptance criteria remain relevant and effective as the project progresses.

To validate and iterate acceptance criteria, teams can conduct regular review sessions with stakeholders, product owners, and development team members. During these sessions, teams discuss acceptance criteria, address any ambiguities or inconsistencies, and make adjustments as needed. Teams can also use feedback from user testing, usability studies, and customer surveys to refine acceptance criteria and prioritize features based on user feedback. By continuously validating and iterating acceptance criteria, teams can adapt to changing requirements, mitigate risks, and deliver software that meets stakeholder expectations.

In summary, acceptance criteria definition is a collaborative process that involves articulating specific conditions and requirements for software acceptance. Effective acceptance criteria are clear, measurable, achievable, and relevant to business objectives and user needs. By defining acceptance criteria early, teams can ensure alignment with project goals, guide development efforts, and deliver high-quality software that meets stakeholder expectations. Collaborative definition, validation, and iteration are key aspects of the acceptance criteria definition process, ensuring that criteria remain accurate and relevant throughout the development lifecycle.

Chapter 10: Test Automation Implementation

Test automation has become an integral part of modern software development processes, revolutionizing the way organizations build, test, and deliver software products. At its core, test automation involves using software tools and scripts to automate the execution of test cases, thereby increasing efficiency, improving test coverage, and accelerating the release cycle. Test automation encompasses various techniques and approaches, including unit testing, functional testing, integration testing, and regression testing, all aimed at automating repetitive testing tasks and ensuring the quality and reliability of software applications. By embracing test automation, organizations can streamline their testing efforts, reduce manual intervention, and achieve faster time-to-market for their products.

Understanding Test Automation Concepts: Test automation involves automating the execution of test cases, scripts, or scenarios using specialized software tools and frameworks. Unlike manual testing, which relies on human testers to execute test cases step by step, test automation leverages automation scripts and tools to perform testing tasks automatically. Test automation frameworks provide a structured approach to writing, organizing, and executing automated tests, enabling testers to achieve repeatability, scalability, and reliability in their testing efforts. Test automation is essential for validating software functionality, detecting defects, and ensuring the stability and performance of software applications across different environments and configurations.

To initiate test automation using Selenium WebDriver, testers can write automated test scripts using programming languages such as Java, Python, or C#. Selenium WebDriver provides a set of APIs for interacting with web elements, performing actions, and validating results. Testers can use commands such as findElement, click, sendKeys, and assert to interact with web elements, simulate user actions, and verify expected outcomes. By writing automation scripts with Selenium WebDriver, testers can automate web application testing, validate software functionality, and identify defects early in the development lifecycle.

Benefits of Test Automation: Test automation offers numerous benefits to organizations, including increased efficiency, improved test coverage, and faster feedback cycles. By automating repetitive testing tasks, organizations can free up valuable time and resources that can be allocated to more strategic activities, such as exploratory testing, code review, and performance optimization. Test automation also enables organizations to achieve higher test coverage by executing a larger number of test cases in a shorter time frame, leading to improved defect detection and reduced risk of regression defects.

To reap the benefits of test automation, organizations can use continuous integration (CI) and continuous delivery (CD) pipelines to automate the execution of automated tests as part of the software build and deployment process. CI/CD pipelines automate the process of building, testing, and deploying software applications, ensuring that changes are validated and integrated into the codebase continuously. Test automation tools such as Jenkins, Travis CI, and CircleCI can be integrated into CI/CD pipelines to execute automated tests automatically whenever changes are made to the codebase. By incorporating test automation into CI/CD pipelines, organizations can achieve faster feedback loops, improve code quality, and deliver software updates to customers more frequently and reliably.

Challenges in Test Automation: Despite its many benefits, test automation also poses several challenges that organizations must address to maximize its effectiveness. One common challenge is the initial investment required to set up and maintain test automation infrastructure, including selecting appropriate tools, frameworks, and technologies, as well as training team members on their use. Additionally, maintaining automated test scripts and keeping them up-to-date with changes in the software application can be challenging, especially in fast-paced development environments where requirements are constantly evolving.

To address these challenges, organizations can adopt best practices for test automation, such as prioritizing test automation efforts based on risk and impact, establishing clear guidelines and standards for writing automation scripts, and investing in tools and technologies that support scalability, maintainability, and extensibility. Organizations can also leverage cloud-based testing platforms and infrastructure-as-code (IaC) tools to automate the provisioning and management of test environments, reducing the overhead associated with maintaining test infrastructure. By adopting a strategic approach to test automation and addressing common challenges proactively, organizations can maximize the return on their investment in test automation and achieve greater efficiency and effectiveness in their testing efforts. **Future Trends in Test Automation:** As software development practices continue to evolve, so too will the field of test automation. Emerging trends such as artificial intelligence (AI) and machine learning (ML) are poised to transform test automation by enabling intelligent test generation, predictive analytics, and autonomous testing capabilities. AI-powered testing tools can analyze historical test data, identify patterns, and recommend optimizations to test suites, helping organizations prioritize testing efforts and improve test coverage. Additionally, advances in containerization and microservices architecture are driving the adoption of container-based testing solutions, which enable organizations to execute tests in isolated, reproducible environments, enhancing reliability and scalability.

To stay ahead of the curve, organizations must embrace these emerging trends and technologies, investing in AI-driven testing tools, container-based testing platforms, and other innovative solutions that enable them to achieve greater automation, efficiency, and agility in their testing practices. By continuously evolving their test automation strategies and embracing new technologies, organizations can keep pace with the demands of modern software development and deliver high-quality software products that meet the needs of their customers and stakeholders.

In summary, test automation is a fundamental aspect of modern software development, enabling organizations to achieve greater efficiency, reliability, and agility in their testing efforts. By understanding the concepts, benefits, challenges, and future trends in test automation, organizations can harness the power of automation to accelerate their release cycles, improve code quality, and deliver superior software products to market.

Selecting the appropriate test automation tools is a crucial step in establishing an efficient and effective test automation strategy. With the proliferation of software testing tools available in the market, choosing the right ones requires careful consideration of various factors, including the project's requirements, team's skillset, supported technologies, and budget constraints. Each test automation tool comes with its own set of features, capabilities, and limitations, making it essential to evaluate and compare multiple options before making a decision. By conducting a thorough assessment and selecting the most suitable tools for the project's needs, teams can streamline test automation efforts, improve test coverage, and accelerate the software development lifecycle.

Understanding Test Automation Tool Landscape: Before delving into the selection process, it's essential to gain a comprehensive understanding of the test automation tool landscape. Test automation tools can be broadly categorized into several types, including record-and-playback tools, scripting-based tools, and framework-based tools. Record-and-playback tools allow testers to record user interactions with the application and replay them as automated tests. Scripting-based tools require testers to write test scripts using programming languages such as Java, Python, or JavaScript. Framework-based tools provide a structured framework for organizing and executing automated tests, offering features such as test case management, reporting, and integration with continuous integration (CI) systems.

To explore the test automation tool landscape, testers can use online resources such as software testing forums, review websites, and vendor websites to research and compare different tools. Tools such as Selenium WebDriver, Appium, and Cypress are popular choices for web application testing, offering robust features for browser automation and cross-browser testing. Tools like TestComplete, Ranorex, and Katalon Studio provide comprehensive test automation solutions for both web and desktop applications, offering features such as object recognition, data-driven testing, and built-in test management capabilities. By familiarizing themselves with the features and capabilities of various test automation tools, teams can make informed decisions during the selection process.

Assessing Project Requirements and Constraints: The selection of test automation tools should be driven by the specific requirements and constraints of the project. Factors to consider include the type of application being tested (web, mobile, desktop), the technology stack used (Java, .NET, JavaScript), the availability of skilled resources, and the project timeline and budget. For example, if the project involves testing a web application built with AngularJS, testers may prefer a test automation tool that offers strong support for AngularJS applications, such as Protractor or TestCafe. Similarly, if the project requires mobile app testing, tools like Appium or Xamarin.UITest may be more suitable.

To assess project requirements and constraints, teams can conduct stakeholder interviews, gather input from developers and testers, and analyze the technical specifications of the application. By understanding the project's unique needs and constraints, teams can narrow down the list of candidate test automation tools and prioritize features that are essential for successful test automation implementation. Additionally, teams should consider factors such as licensing costs, maintenance overhead, and scalability when evaluating test automation tools, ensuring that the selected tools align with the project's budget and long-term goals.

Evaluating Features and Capabilities: Once the project requirements are defined, teams can begin evaluating test automation tools based on their features, capabilities, and suitability for the project. Key features to consider include support for multiple platforms and technologies, ease of test script creation and maintenance, integration with existing tools and frameworks, reporting and analytics capabilities, and scalability for large test suites. Additionally, teams should assess the tool's support for test automation best practices such as data-driven testing, keyword-driven testing, and behavior-driven development (BDD).

To evaluate test automation tools, teams can create a list of evaluation criteria and score each tool against those criteria. Tools such as Test Automation Framework Evaluation (TAFE) and Test Automation Matrix (TAM) provide structured frameworks for evaluating and comparing test automation tools based on predefined criteria such as functionality, usability, performance, and support. Teams can also conduct proof-of-concept (POC) exercises or pilot projects using selected tools to assess their suitability and effectiveness in real-world scenarios. By systematically evaluating features and capabilities, teams can identify the test automation tools that best meet their needs and objectives.

Considering Long-Term Viability and Support: In addition to features and capabilities, teams should also consider the long-term viability and support of the selected test automation tools. Factors to consider include the vendor's reputation and track record, the tool's user community and ecosystem, the frequency of updates and releases, and the availability of technical support and documentation. Choosing a tool with strong vendor support and a vibrant user community can provide valuable resources and assistance throughout the test automation implementation and maintenance process.

To assess the long-term viability and support of test automation tools, teams can research vendor websites, read user reviews and testimonials, and participate in online forums and discussion groups. They can also reach out to vendor representatives to inquire about support options, training programs, and future roadmap plans. By selecting a test automation tool with a solid reputation and strong vendor support, teams can minimize risks and ensure the long-term success of their test automation initiatives.

Finalizing Selection and Implementation: Once the evaluation process is complete, teams can finalize their selection of test automation tools and proceed with implementation. This involves setting up the selected tools, configuring test environments, creating test scripts, and integrating test automation into the continuous integration (CI) pipeline. Teams should establish best practices and guidelines for test automation development, including coding standards, version control practices, and test script organization.

To implement test automation effectively, teams can leverage CLI commands and automation scripts to streamline deployment and configuration tasks. For example, tools like Selenium WebDriver provide CLI commands for installing browser drivers and executing automated tests from the command line interface. Similarly, CI/CD platforms such as Jenkins and GitLab CI offer CLI commands for automating build and deployment processes, enabling seamless integration of test automation into the software development lifecycle. By leveraging CLI commands and automation scripts, teams can automate repetitive tasks, reduce manual effort, and increase the efficiency of test automation implementation.

In summary, selecting test automation tools requires a systematic approach that considers project requirements, evaluates features and capabilities, assesses long-term viability and support, and involves stakeholders throughout the process. By following best practices and leveraging CLI commands and automation scripts, teams can streamline the selection and implementation of test automation tools, enabling efficient and effective software testing practices.

BOOK 3
DEBUGGING PLAYBOOK
ADVANCED STRATEGIES FOR VULNERABILITY
REMEDIATION

ROB BOTWRIGHT

Chapter 1: Introduction to Error Localization

Error localization is a critical aspect of software development and debugging, playing a pivotal role in identifying and resolving issues that arise during the development lifecycle. It refers to the process of pinpointing the root cause of errors or defects in software applications, enabling developers to understand why the errors occurred and how to fix them effectively. The importance of error localization cannot be overstated, as it directly impacts the quality, reliability, and performance of software systems. By accurately localizing errors, developers can expedite the debugging process, reduce downtime, and enhance the overall user experience. Effective error localization requires a systematic approach, leveraging various techniques and tools to isolate and diagnose software defects efficiently.

Enhancing Software Reliability: One of the primary reasons error localization is essential is its role in enhancing the reliability and stability of software systems. Software applications are prone to errors and defects due to factors such as coding errors, software dependencies, environmental factors, and user interactions. Without proper error localization, these errors can propagate throughout the system, leading to system crashes, data corruption, and loss of functionality. By localizing errors accurately, developers can identify the underlying causes and implement targeted fixes to address them, thereby improving the reliability and robustness of the software.

To enhance software reliability through error localization, developers can use CLI commands such as debugging tools and logging utilities to trace the execution flow of the software and identify potential error sources. For example, tools like GDB (GNU Debugger) and LLDB (LLVM Debugger) allow developers to analyze program execution, inspect variables, and identify memory-related issues through command-line interfaces. Similarly, logging libraries such as Log4j and Serilog enable developers to log relevant information and diagnostic messages to facilitate error localization and troubleshooting.

Minimizing Downtime and Disruption: Another key benefit of error localization is its ability to minimize downtime and disruption in software systems. When errors occur in production environments, they can have a significant impact on business operations, leading to service interruptions, revenue loss, and reputational damage. Rapid identification and localization of errors are crucial for mitigating these risks and restoring normal operations promptly. By isolating the root cause of errors quickly, developers can implement targeted fixes and deploy patches or updates to resolve the issues without causing prolonged downtime or disruption to end-users.

To minimize downtime and disruption, developers can use CLI commands such as system monitoring tools and error tracking utilities to detect and diagnose errors in real-time. For example, tools like Nagios and Zabbix provide command-line interfaces for monitoring system performance, alerting developers to potential issues such as high CPU usage, memory leaks, or network failures. Error tracking platforms such as Sentry and Raygun offer CLI commands for capturing and aggregating error logs and crash reports, enabling developers to identify patterns and trends in error occurrences across distributed systems.

Improving User Experience: Error localization plays a crucial role in improving the overall user experience of software applications. User-facing errors such as crashes, freezes, and unexpected behavior can frustrate users and erode their confidence in the software. By localizing and fixing these errors promptly, developers can enhance user satisfaction, loyalty, and retention. Moreover, transparent error handling and informative error messages can help users understand the nature of the problem and take appropriate actions to mitigate its impact.

To improve the user experience through error localization, developers can leverage CLI commands such as error monitoring tools and user feedback mechanisms to gather insights into user-reported issues and prioritize error resolution efforts. For example, tools like Bugsnag and Rollbar offer command-line interfaces for collecting and analyzing error reports from production environments, enabling developers to identify recurring issues and address them proactively. User feedback channels such as in-app feedback forms, support tickets, and community forums provide valuable insights into user pain points and usability issues, guiding developers in prioritizing error localization efforts based on user impact and severity.

Facilitating Continuous Improvement: Error localization serves as a foundation for continuous improvement in software development processes and practices. By analyzing and addressing errors systematically, teams can identify areas for process improvement, enhance code quality, and prevent similar errors from occurring in the future. Moreover, error localization fosters a culture of accountability, collaboration, and learning within development teams, encouraging proactive problem-solving and knowledge sharing.

To facilitate continuous improvement through error localization, teams can use CLI commands such as version control systems and issue tracking platforms to manage and track error resolution efforts over time. For example, tools like Git and SVN provide command-line interfaces for branching, merging, and committing code changes, enabling developers to collaborate on error fixes and review code changes efficiently. Issue tracking platforms such as Jira and GitHub Issues offer CLI commands for creating, assigning, and updating issues related to error reports and bug fixes, facilitating transparency and accountability in the error resolution process.

In summary, error localization is of paramount importance in software development, contributing to enhanced reliability, minimized downtime, improved user experience, and facilitated continuous improvement. By leveraging CLI commands and adopting a systematic approach to error localization, developers can identify and address software defects effectively, ultimately leading to more robust, stable, and user-friendly software applications.

Error localization, despite its critical importance in software development, presents numerous challenges that developers must navigate to effectively identify and resolve issues. These challenges span various aspects of the development lifecycle, from understanding the nature of errors to implementing solutions that address them comprehensively. By acknowledging and addressing these challenges, developers can streamline the error localization process and ensure the timely delivery of high-quality software products.

Ambiguous Error Symptoms: One of the primary challenges in error localization is dealing with ambiguous error symptoms that provide limited information about the underlying cause of the issue. When errors manifest as generic error messages or unexpected behavior without clear context, developers face difficulty in pinpointing the root cause. For example, a web application may display a

"500 Internal Server Error" message without indicating which specific component or function failed.

To address ambiguous error symptoms, developers can use CLI commands such as log analysis tools and debugging utilities to gather additional information about error occurrences. For instance, tailing log files using the **tail** command in Unix-based systems or the **Get-Content** command in Windows PowerShell can provide real-time insights into application errors, allowing developers to identify patterns and trends. Additionally, enabling verbose logging and error reporting in the application configuration settings can help capture more detailed diagnostic information for analysis.

Reproducibility of Errors: Another common challenge in error localization is the reproducibility of errors, especially those that occur sporadically or under specific conditions. When errors occur inconsistently or cannot be replicated reliably, developers may struggle to diagnose and resolve them effectively. Factors such as environmental differences, concurrency issues, and timing dependencies can contribute to the unpredictability of error occurrences.

To address the reproducibility of errors, developers can use CLI commands such as version control systems and virtualization tools to create isolated testing environments that replicate the conditions under which errors occur. For example, using Git to create a feature branch and Docker to containerize the application environment can help standardize the testing environment across different development and deployment stages. By isolating variables and controlling external factors, developers can increase the likelihood of reproducing errors consistently and analyzing them in a controlled setting.

Complexity of Distributed Systems: In modern software architectures, distributed systems composed of microservices, APIs, and third-party integrations introduce additional complexity to the error localization process. Errors in distributed systems can propagate across multiple components and layers, making it challenging to trace their origins and dependencies. Moreover, issues such as network latency, service dependencies, and asynchronous communication further complicate error localization efforts.

To address the complexity of distributed systems, developers can use CLI commands such as network monitoring tools and distributed tracing utilities to trace the flow of requests and responses across interconnected services. For example, using tools like Wireshark or tcpdump to capture network traffic can provide insights into communication patterns and identify potential bottlenecks or errors. Similarly, incorporating distributed tracing frameworks like Jaeger or Zipkin into the application architecture can enable end-to-end visibility into transaction flows and service interactions, facilitating error localization and performance optimization.

Limited Visibility in Production Environments: Obtaining visibility into error occurrences and system behavior in production environments poses a significant challenge for developers, as production environments often have limited access and monitoring capabilities. Errors that occur in production may go unnoticed or unreported, leading to prolonged downtime and user dissatisfaction. Additionally, concerns about data privacy and security may restrict the collection and transmission of error-related information from production systems.

To address limited visibility in production environments, developers can use CLI commands such as remote logging tools and error monitoring platforms to capture and analyze error data without impacting production performance. For example, configuring centralized logging using tools like ELK

Stack (Elasticsearch, Logstash, Kibana) or Splunk can aggregate log data from distributed systems and provide real-time insights into error occurrences. Similarly, integrating error monitoring platforms such as Sentry or Rollbar into the application codebase can automatically capture and report errors to a centralized dashboard for analysis and resolution.

Dependency Management and Compatibility Issues: Dependencies on third-party libraries, frameworks, and services introduce additional challenges in error localization, particularly when compatibility issues arise between different versions or configurations. Changes in dependencies can introduce unforeseen bugs or conflicts that manifest as errors in the software application. Moreover, managing dependencies across different environments (development, staging, production) adds complexity to the error localization process.

To address dependency management and compatibility issues, developers can use CLI commands such as package managers and dependency analysis tools to track and manage dependencies effectively. For example, using package managers like npm (Node.js Package Manager) or pip (Python Package Installer) to install and manage dependencies can ensure consistency and reproducibility across different environments. Additionally, leveraging dependency analysis tools such as OWASP Dependency-Check or Snyk can identify security vulnerabilities and outdated dependencies in the software stack, enabling proactive mitigation and risk management.

Cross-Platform and Cross-Browser Compatibility: Ensuring compatibility across different platforms and browsers presents a significant challenge in error localization, particularly for web applications and mobile apps. Variations in browser rendering engines, operating system configurations, and device characteristics can lead to inconsistencies and compatibility issues that manifest as errors or unexpected behavior. Moreover, the proliferation of mobile devices with diverse screen sizes, resolutions, and hardware capabilities further complicates the testing and localization of errors.

To address cross-platform and cross-browser compatibility challenges, developers can use CLI commands such as browser automation tools and device emulators to test applications across multiple platforms and configurations. For example, using Selenium WebDriver with WebDriver-based browser drivers (e.g., ChromeDriver, GeckoDriver) allows developers to automate browser testing and execute test scripts across different browsers and platforms. Similarly, using mobile device emulators or simulators provided by platforms like Android Studio or Xcode enables developers to test mobile applications on virtual devices with varying configurations.

Time and Resource Constraints: Finally, time and resource constraints pose significant challenges in error localization, as developers often face pressure to diagnose and resolve errors within tight deadlines and limited resources. Balancing competing priorities and allocating resources effectively to error localization efforts can be challenging, particularly in fast-paced development environments where speed to market is critical. Moreover, addressing complex or elusive errors may require extensive time and effort, further exacerbating resource constraints.

To address time and resource constraints, developers can use CLI commands such as task automation tools and continuous integration (CI) pipelines to streamline error localization processes and automate repetitive tasks. For example, using task runners like npm scripts or Makefiles to automate common tasks such as running tests, building artifacts, and deploying applications can save time and reduce manual effort. Similarly, integrating error tracking and reporting tools into CI pipelines using platforms like Jenkins, GitLab CI, or Travis CI can facilitate early detection and resolution of errors during the development and deployment phases.

In summary, error localization presents numerous challenges that developers must navigate to ensure the timely delivery of high-quality software products. By acknowledging these challenges and adopting effective strategies and tools, developers can streamline the error localization process, mitigate risks, and deliver software solutions that meet user expectations and business objectives.

Chapter 2: Log Analysis Methods

Log files serve as invaluable sources of information for developers, administrators, and system operators, providing insights into the behavior, performance, and health of software applications and systems. Understanding the structure and formats of log files is essential for effectively analyzing and troubleshooting issues that arise during software development, deployment, and operation. Log files typically consist of timestamped entries or messages that record various events, errors, warnings, and diagnostic information generated by the software or operating system. These entries follow specific formats dictated by logging frameworks, protocols, or conventions, which vary depending on the platform, programming language, and logging standards adopted by the application or system.

Timestamps and Event Sequencing: Timestamps play a crucial role in log file structure, providing chronological context for events and entries recorded in the log. Timestamps indicate when each event occurred, allowing developers and operators to correlate events, identify patterns, and analyze system behavior over time. Common timestamp formats include ISO 8601 (e.g., "YYYY-MM-DDTHH:MM:SSZ"), Unix epoch time (e.g., milliseconds since January 1, 1970), and human-readable date-time strings (e.g., "Mon Jan 02 15:04:05 -0700 2006"). By standardizing timestamp formats, log files enable consistent interpretation and comparison of time-sensitive information across different systems and environments.

To view timestamped entries in log files, developers can use CLI commands such as **grep**, **awk**, or **sed** to filter and extract entries based on specific date ranges or time intervals. For example, to display log entries between two timestamps using **grep**, developers can use the following command:

perlCopy code

```
grep '2022-01-01T00:00:00Z' logfile.txt | grep '2022-01-02T00:00:00Z'
```

This command filters entries containing timestamps within the specified range, allowing developers to focus on relevant events within a specific timeframe.

Message Severity Levels: Log entries often include severity levels or priorities that indicate the importance or criticality of each event recorded in the log. Common severity levels include DEBUG, INFO, WARN (or WARNING), ERROR, and FATAL (or CRITICAL), which represent different levels of urgency or significance. DEBUG messages provide detailed diagnostic information for debugging purposes, while INFO messages convey general status updates or operational information. WARN and ERROR messages indicate potential issues or errors that require attention, with ERROR messages representing more critical failures that may impact system functionality. FATAL messages signify severe errors or conditions that result in system-wide failures or crashes.

To filter log entries based on severity levels, developers can use CLI commands such as **grep** or **awk** to select entries with specific severity levels. For example, to display ERROR messages from a log file using **grep**, developers can use the following command:

perlCopy code

```
grep 'ERROR' logfile.txt
```

This command filters entries containing the string "ERROR," allowing developers to focus on identifying and addressing critical errors recorded in the log.

Message Formats and Structured Logging: Log entries may adhere to predefined formats or schemas that define the structure and content of each message. Structured logging formats, such as JSON (JavaScript Object Notation) or XML (eXtensible Markup Language), enable developers to organize log data into key-value pairs or hierarchical structures, facilitating automated parsing, analysis, and processing. Structured logging enhances readability, searchability, and interoperability of log data across different systems and tools, enabling more efficient log analysis and integration with monitoring and analytics platforms.

To parse structured log entries, developers can use CLI commands such as **jq** (for JSON data) or **xmlstarlet** (for XML data) to extract specific fields or properties from log messages. For example, to extract the "message" field from JSON-formatted log entries using **jq**, developers can use the following command:

arduinoCopy code

```
jq '.message' logfile.json
```

This command extracts the "message" field from each JSON object in the log file, allowing developers to retrieve relevant information contained within structured log entries.

Log Rotation and Archiving: Log files often undergo rotation and archiving to manage file size, disk space usage, and retention policies. Log rotation involves periodically renaming or compressing log files and creating new empty files to continue logging events. Archiving involves storing older log files in compressed or encrypted archives for long-term storage or compliance purposes. Log rotation and archiving strategies vary depending on factors such as log volume, retention requirements, and regulatory compliance mandates.

To perform log rotation and archiving tasks, developers can use CLI commands such as **logrotate** or **tar** to automate the process and manage log files efficiently. For example, using the **logrotate** command with a configuration file (**logrotate.conf**) allows developers to define rotation policies and schedules for log files. Similarly, using the **tar** command with compression options (**-czvf**) enables developers to create compressed archives of log files for storage or backup purposes.

Custom Log Formats and Configuration: Some applications or systems allow customization of log formats and configuration settings to tailor logging behavior according to specific requirements or preferences. Custom log formats enable developers to include additional metadata, context, or diagnostic information in log entries, enhancing the granularity and richness of log data. Configuration options may include log output destinations, log levels, log file rotation policies, and log retention settings, providing flexibility and control over logging behavior.

To configure custom log formats and settings, developers can use CLI commands to modify configuration files or interact with logging frameworks or libraries programmatically. For example, using the **sed** command to modify a configuration file (**log4j.properties**) allows developers to customize logging settings such as log file paths, log levels, and output formats. Similarly, using environment variables or command-line arguments to override default logging configurations enables developers to adapt logging behavior dynamically based on runtime conditions or deployment environments.

In summary, understanding the structure and formats of log files is essential for effective log analysis, troubleshooting, and monitoring in software development and operations. By leveraging CLI commands and logging best practices, developers can extract actionable insights from log data, diagnose issues efficiently, and ensure the reliability and performance of software applications and systems.

Chapter 3: Debugging Tools Overview

Debugging tools are essential assets for software developers, aiding in the identification and resolution of issues throughout the development lifecycle. These tools come in various forms, each serving specific purposes and catering to different aspects of the debugging process. From basic utilities for inspecting code execution to sophisticated profilers for performance analysis, understanding the types and functionalities of debugging tools is crucial for effective troubleshooting and problem-solving.

Interactive Debuggers: Interactive debuggers are foundational tools for code inspection and execution analysis. They enable developers to step through code line by line, set breakpoints, and inspect variables and memory contents during runtime. CLI-based debuggers such as GDB (GNU Debugger) and LLDB (LLVM Debugger) provide command-line interfaces for debugging C, C++, and other compiled languages. These tools allow developers to control program execution, examine call stacks, and diagnose logic errors and memory issues interactively.

To debug a C program using GDB, developers can compile the program with debugging symbols (**-g** flag) and launch GDB with the executable file as an argument. For example:

bashCopy code

gcc -g -o my_program my_program.c gdb ./my_program

Static Code Analyzers: Static code analyzers examine source code without executing it, identifying potential errors, vulnerabilities, and code smells based on predefined rules and patterns. These tools help detect common programming mistakes, security vulnerabilities, and maintainability issues early in the development process, reducing the likelihood of bugs and security flaws in the deployed software. CLI-based static analyzers such as Clang Static Analyzer and Pylint analyze C/C++ and Python code respectively, providing actionable feedback and suggestions for code improvement.

To perform static code analysis on a Python script using Pylint, developers can install Pylint using pip and run it on the script file. For example:

Copy code

```
pip install pylint pylint my_script.py
```

Dynamic Analysis Tools: Dynamic analysis tools monitor program behavior during execution, capturing runtime information such as memory usage, CPU utilization, and function call traces. These tools help identify performance bottlenecks, resource leaks, and unexpected behavior in real-world scenarios. CLI-based dynamic analysis tools such as Valgrind (for memory debugging) and strace (for system call tracing) provide insights into program execution at the system level, enabling developers to diagnose low-level issues and optimize application performance.

To perform memory debugging on a C program using Valgrind, developers can compile the program with debugging symbols and run it through Valgrind's memcheck tool. For example:

bashCopy code

```
gcc -g -o my_program my_program.c valgrind --leak-
check=full ./my_program
```

Performance Profilers: Performance profilers analyze program performance by measuring resource usage, execution time, and function call frequencies. These tools help developers identify performance bottlenecks, optimize code, and improve overall system efficiency. CLI-based profilers such as perf (Linux Performance Tools) and gprof (GNU Profiler) offer insights into CPU usage, memory allocation, and function call graphs, allowing developers to pinpoint areas of code that contribute most to performance overhead.

To profile a C program using gprof, developers can compile the program with profiling options and run it to generate profiling data. For example:

bashCopy code

```
gcc -pg -o my_program my_program.c ./my_program
gprof ./my_program
```

Debugging Frameworks and Libraries: Debugging frameworks and libraries provide developers with reusable components and APIs for instrumenting, tracing, and debugging software applications. These tools offer advanced debugging capabilities, such as remote debugging, logging, and error monitoring, and can be integrated into development workflows and toolchains. CLI-based debugging libraries such as logging frameworks (e.g., Log4j for Java, loguru for Python) and error monitoring platforms (e.g., Sentry, Rollbar) enable developers to instrument code for diagnostic purposes and capture runtime information for analysis and troubleshooting.

To integrate error monitoring into a Python application using Sentry, developers can install the Sentry SDK using pip and initialize it with the appropriate configuration. For example:

Copy code

```
pip install sentry-sdk
```

Network Debugging Tools: Network debugging tools assist developers in diagnosing issues related to network communication, such as packet loss, latency, and protocol errors. These tools capture and analyze network traffic, monitor network connections, and troubleshoot connectivity issues between distributed systems. CLI-based network debugging tools such as tcpdump (packet capture tool) and Wireshark (network protocol analyzer) provide visibility into network activity and enable developers to inspect packet payloads, analyze protocol interactions, and identify anomalies or performance bottlenecks.

To capture network traffic using tcpdump, developers can specify network interfaces and filtering criteria to capture relevant packets. For example:

cssCopy code

```
tcpdump -i eth0 -n host 192.168.1.1
```

In summary, the diverse range of debugging tools available to developers offers comprehensive support for identifying, analyzing, and resolving issues encountered during software development and operation. By leveraging CLI-based debugging tools and integrating them into development workflows, developers can streamline the debugging process, improve code quality, and deliver robust and reliable software solutions.

Choosing the right debugging tool for the job is a critical decision that can significantly impact the efficiency and effectiveness of the debugging process. With a plethora of debugging tools available, ranging from interactive debuggers to static analyzers and performance profilers, developers must consider various factors such as the nature of the problem, the programming language used, and the desired level of analysis and insight. By evaluating the specific requirements and constraints of the debugging task, developers can select the most suitable tool to diagnose and resolve issues promptly and accurately.

Nature of the Problem: The nature of the problem at hand plays a pivotal role in determining the appropriate debugging tool. For logic errors and runtime issues, interactive debuggers like GDB and LLDB are invaluable, allowing developers to step through code, inspect variables, and analyze program behavior in real-time. Conversely, for identifying code defects and vulnerabilities at the source code level, static code analyzers such as Pylint and Clang Static Analyzer offer static analysis capabilities to detect potential errors and security flaws without executing the code.

To debug a C program using GDB, developers can compile the program with debugging symbols and launch GDB with the executable file as an argument:

bashCopy code

```
gcc -g -o my_program my_program.c gdb ./my_program
```

Programming Language Support: The choice of debugging tool is often influenced by the programming language used in the development project. While some debugging tools are language-agnostic and support multiple programming languages, others are tailored specifically for particular languages or language ecosystems. For instance, Python developers may prefer tools like PDB (Python Debugger) and pdb++ for debugging Python code, while C and C++ developers may rely on GDB or Valgrind for debugging compiled binaries.

To debug a Python script using PDB, developers can launch the script with PDB as the interpreter, allowing them to interactively debug the code:

Copy code

```
python -m pdb my_script.py
```

Level of Analysis and Insight: Different debugging tools offer varying levels of analysis and insight into program behavior, ranging from low-level memory debugging to high-level performance profiling. Developers must consider the depth and granularity of analysis required to diagnose the issue effectively. For memory-related issues and resource leaks, dynamic analysis tools like Valgrind's memcheck provide detailed memory usage information and detect memory-related errors such as invalid memory accesses and memory leaks.

To perform memory debugging on a C program using Valgrind, developers can compile the program with debugging symbols and run it through Valgrind's memcheck tool:

bashCopy code

```
gcc -g -o my_program my_program.c valgrind --leak-check=full ./my_program
```

Tool Integration and Compatibility: Integration with existing development workflows and toolchains is another crucial consideration when choosing a debugging tool.

Developers should assess the compatibility and interoperability of debugging tools with other development tools, version control systems, and CI/CD pipelines. Tools that seamlessly integrate with IDEs (Integrated Development Environments) and version control platforms enhance developer productivity and streamline the debugging process by providing seamless access to debugging features within familiar development environments.

To integrate GDB with an IDE like Visual Studio Code (VS Code), developers can install the "C/C++" extension and configure the debugger to use GDB as the backend debugger:

Copy code

```
ext install ms-vscode.cpptools
```

Community Support and Documentation: Community support and documentation are essential factors to consider when evaluating debugging tools. Robust community support ensures timely assistance and access to resources such as tutorials, forums, and documentation, facilitating the learning curve and troubleshooting process for developers. Tools with active community forums, online documentation, and comprehensive user guides empower developers to leverage the full potential of debugging tools and address complex debugging challenges effectively.

To seek assistance or share knowledge with the GDB community, developers can visit the official GDB mailing lists or forums:

arduinoCopy code

```
https://www.sourceware.org/lists.html
```

Scalability and Performance: Scalability and performance considerations are paramount, especially when dealing with large codebases or performance-sensitive applications. Developers should assess the scalability and performance overhead of debugging tools to ensure minimal impact on application performance and resource utilization during debugging sessions. Tools that offer efficient resource utilization, minimal runtime overhead, and support for multi-threaded and distributed applications are preferable for debugging complex and performance-critical systems.

To profile a C program using gprof, developers can compile the program with profiling options and run it to generate profiling data:

bashCopy code

```
gcc -pg -o my_program my_program.c ./my_program
gprof ./my_program
```

In summary, choosing the right debugging tool requires careful consideration of various factors, including the nature of the problem, programming language support, level of analysis, tool integration, community support, and performance considerations. By selecting the most suitable debugging tool for the task at hand, developers can streamline the debugging process, accelerate issue resolution, and deliver high-quality software solutions.

Chapter 4: Understanding Stack Traces

Understanding the anatomy of a stack trace is crucial for effective debugging and error diagnosis in software development. A stack trace provides valuable information about the sequence of function calls and execution contexts leading to an exception or error condition. By analyzing the components and structure of a stack trace, developers can pinpoint the origin of errors, trace the execution flow, and identify the root cause of issues more efficiently.

Function Call Chain: At the core of a stack trace is the function call chain, which represents the sequence of function invocations leading to the occurrence of an error. Each entry in the stack trace corresponds to a function call, with the most recent invocation appearing at the top of the stack and the initial invocation (usually the entry point of the program) at the bottom. The function names, along with their associated source code files and line numbers, provide context about the execution flow and the path taken by the program leading up to the error.

To generate a stack trace in Python when an exception occurs, developers can use the traceback module to print the traceback information:

pythonCopy code

```
import traceback try: # Code that may raise an exception ...
except Exception: traceback.print_exc()
```

File Paths and Line Numbers: Stack traces typically include file paths and line numbers associated with each function call, facilitating the identification of the source code locations where errors occurred. This information helps developers navigate to the relevant code sections quickly and inspect the context surrounding the error. By examining the specific lines of code referenced in the stack trace, developers can gain insights into the conditions and variables leading to the error condition.

In Java, developers can use the **printStackTrace()** method of the Throwable class to print a stack trace:

javaCopy code

```
try { // Code that may throw an exception ... } catch (Exception e) { e.printStackTrace(); }
```

Exception Type and Message: Alongside the function call chain, stack traces include information about the type of exception or error encountered, along with an optional error message providing additional context about the nature of the error. Exception types such as NullPointerException, IndexError, or Segmentation Fault (in lower-level languages like C/C++) convey the specific nature of the error condition, while error messages offer descriptive explanations or diagnostic clues to aid in debugging.

In JavaScript, developers can use the **console.error()** method to log an error message along with a stack trace:

javascriptCopy code

```
try { // Code that may throw an error ... } catch (error) { console.error("An error occurred:", error); }
```

Nested Stack Frames: In scenarios where function calls are nested within one another (e.g., recursive functions or callbacks), stack traces include multiple nested stack frames, each representing a distinct level of the call hierarchy. Nested stack frames provide visibility into the execution context at each level of recursion or callback invocation, allowing developers to trace the execution flow across multiple function boundaries and identify potential issues arising from nested function interactions.

In Ruby, developers can use the **backtrace** method of the Exception class to access the array of backtrace lines representing the stack trace:

rubyCopy code

```
begin # Code that may raise an exception ... rescue Exception => e puts e.backtrace end
```

Stack Frame Metadata: Stack traces may include additional metadata associated with each stack frame, such as the memory addresses of function calls, register states, or optimization information (in compiled languages). While this level of detail may not always be necessary for routine debugging tasks, it can be valuable in certain scenarios, such as low-level debugging or performance optimization, where developers need insights into the underlying system behavior and execution environment.

In C/C++, developers can use the **backtrace()** function along with the **backtrace_symbols()** function to obtain symbolic names for the stack frames:

cppCopy code

```
#include <execinfo.h> #include <iostream> void printStackTrace() { void* stackFrames[10]; int numFrames = backtrace(stackFrames, 10); char** symbols = backtrace_symbols(stackFrames, numFrames); for (int i = 0; i < numFrames; ++i) { std::cout << symbols[i] << std::endl; } free(symbols); }
```

By dissecting the components of a stack trace and leveraging appropriate tools and techniques for stack trace analysis, developers can gain valuable insights into the runtime behavior of their applications, diagnose errors effectively, and implement targeted fixes to enhance software reliability and robustness.

Interpreting stack trace information is a fundamental skill for software developers, as it provides critical insights into the runtime behavior of applications and aids in diagnosing errors and exceptions effectively. Stack traces contain valuable details about the sequence of function calls leading up to an error, including function names, file paths, line numbers, and exception types. By understanding how to interpret stack trace information, developers can navigate through the call stack, identify the root cause of issues, and implement appropriate fixes to enhance application stability and reliability.

Analyzing Function Call Sequence: At the core of interpreting a stack trace is analyzing the function call sequence, which represents the sequence of nested function invocations leading to the occurrence of an error or exception. Each entry in the stack trace corresponds to a function call, with the most recent invocation appearing at the top of the stack. By examining the order of function calls in the stack trace, developers can trace the execution flow of the program and understand the sequence of events that led to the error condition.

In Python, developers can use the built-in **traceback** module to analyze stack traces and extract information about the function call sequence:

pythonCopy code

```
import traceback try: # Code that may raise an exception ...
except Exception: traceback.print_exc()
```

Identifying Error Context: Stack traces provide contextual information about the location and context in which an error occurred, including file paths and line numbers associated with each function call. By examining the file paths and line numbers referenced in the stack trace, developers can pinpoint the specific lines of code where errors occurred and gain insights into the conditions and variables contributing to the error condition.

In Java, developers can leverage the **printStackTrace()** method of the Throwable class to print stack traces and analyze error context:

javaCopy code

```
try { // Code that may throw an exception ... } catch (Exception e) { e.printStackTrace(); }
```

Understanding Exception Types: Stack traces include information about the type of exception or error encountered during program execution, providing insights into the nature of the error condition. Exception types such as NullPointerException, IndexError, or FileNotFoundError convey specific information about the type of error encountered, helping developers diagnose and address the underlying issues more effectively.

In JavaScript, developers can use the **console.error()** method to log error messages along with stack traces and understand exception types:

javascriptCopy code

```
try { // Code that may throw an error ... } catch (error) { console.error("An error occurred:", error); }
```

Tracing Execution Flow: Stack traces allow developers to trace the execution flow of their applications across multiple function boundaries and execution contexts. By analyzing the sequence of function calls and their associated contexts, developers can gain visibility into the path taken by the program leading up to the error condition, enabling them to identify potential bottlenecks, edge cases, or unexpected behaviors.

In Ruby, developers can use the **backtrace** method of the Exception class to access the array of backtrace lines representing the stack trace and trace the execution flow:

rubyCopy code

```
begin # Code that may raise an exception ... rescue
Exception => e puts e.backtrace end
```

Debugging and Troubleshooting: Interpreting stack trace information is an essential part of the debugging and troubleshooting process, allowing developers to diagnose errors, isolate problematic code segments, and implement targeted fixes. By carefully analyzing stack traces and correlating them with the corresponding source code, developers can expedite the debugging process and ensure the stability and reliability of their applications.

In C/C++, developers can use the **backtrace()** function along with the **backtrace_symbols()** function to obtain symbolic names for the stack frames and troubleshoot issues:

cppCopy code

```
#include <execinfo.h> #include <iostream> void
printStackTrace() { void * stackFrames[10]; int numFrames
= backtrace(stackFrames, 10); char** symbols =
backtrace_symbols(stackFrames, numFrames); for (int i =
0; i < numFrames; ++i) { std::cout << symbols[i] << std::endl;
} free(symbols); }
```

By mastering the art of interpreting stack trace information, developers can streamline the debugging process, diagnose errors with precision, and ensure the reliability and robustness of their software applications.

Chapter 5: Code Review Techniques

The code review process is a critical aspect of software development, aimed at ensuring code quality, fostering collaboration, and mitigating potential issues before they impact production environments. At its core, code review involves systematically examining source code changes to identify defects, improve readability, and maintain consistency with coding standards and best practices. The process typically involves multiple stakeholders, including developers, team leads, and sometimes external reviewers, who collectively assess the code changes for correctness, efficiency, and adherence to project requirements.

Initiating a Code Review: The code review process begins when a developer completes a set of changes or new features and submits them for review. In many version control systems like Git, initiating a code review involves creating a pull request (PR) or merge request (MR) that includes the proposed code changes. The developer assigns the review to one or more team members, who are responsible for evaluating the changes and providing feedback.

To initiate a code review using Git, developers typically create a new branch for their changes, commit the modifications, and push the branch to the remote repository. Then, they create a pull request using the Git hosting platform's interface, such as GitHub or GitLab:

bashCopy code

```
git checkout -b feature-branch # Make changes to the
code git add . git commit -m "Implement new feature" git
push origin feature-branch
```

Reviewing Code Changes: Once a code review is initiated, reviewers examine the proposed changes in detail, focusing on aspects such as code logic, architecture, readability, and adherence to coding standards. Reviewers inspect the diff of the changes, compare them against the original codebase, and analyze the impact of the modifications on the overall system. They may also run tests locally to validate the functionality and verify that the changes integrate seamlessly with the existing codebase.

Reviewers can use various tools and techniques to review code changes effectively. For instance, they may utilize integrated code review features provided by version control platforms or code review tools like Gerrit or Phabricator. Additionally, automated code analysis tools can assist reviewers in identifying potential issues, such as code style violations, security vulnerabilities, or performance bottlenecks.

Providing Feedback: During the code review process, reviewers provide feedback to the author regarding areas that require improvement or correction. Feedback may include suggestions for refactoring code, clarifications on implementation decisions, or requests for additional tests or documentation. Reviewers strive to offer constructive criticism aimed at enhancing the quality of the codebase and fostering continuous improvement within the development team.

To provide feedback on a code review in GitHub, reviewers can add comments directly on specific lines of code within the pull request interface. They can also request changes or approve the pull request based on their assessment of the code changes. Similarly, other code review platforms offer similar features for providing feedback and collaboration.

Iterative Review Process: The code review process is often iterative, with authors addressing feedback from reviewers through subsequent revisions of the code. Authors revise their code based on the feedback received, incorporating suggested improvements, addressing concerns, and ensuring alignment with project requirements. Reviewers then reevaluate the updated code changes, providing additional feedback as needed until consensus is reached on the quality and readiness of the code for integration.

Iterative code review cycles help ensure that code changes undergo thorough scrutiny and refinement, resulting in higher-quality software deliverables. By embracing an iterative approach to code review, teams can foster a culture of collaboration, knowledge sharing, and continuous improvement, leading to more robust and maintainable codebases.

Approving and Merging Changes: Once reviewers are satisfied with the quality of the code changes and all feedback has been addressed, the code review concludes with the approval of the pull request. The author or designated approver merges the approved changes into the main codebase, incorporating the new features or bug fixes into the project's development branch or main branch. The merged code undergoes further testing, validation, and deployment processes before being released to production environments.

In Git-based workflows, merging a pull request typically involves navigating to the pull request interface on the Git hosting platform and clicking the merge button. This action merges the changes into the target branch, triggering automated build and test pipelines to ensure the integrity of the merged code.

The code review process is an indispensable aspect of modern software development methodologies, enabling teams to uphold code quality, foster collaboration, and deliver high-quality software products to end users. By following established code review best practices and leveraging appropriate tools and techniques, development teams can streamline the review process, mitigate potential issues, and achieve greater efficiency and effectiveness in their software development workflows.

Effective code reviews are essential for maintaining code quality, fostering collaboration, and improving overall development processes within a software development team. By adhering to best practices, teams can maximize the benefits of code reviews and ensure that they contribute positively to the development lifecycle. Here, we delve into some of the key best practices for conducting efficient and productive code reviews.

Set Clear Objectives and Guidelines: Establishing clear objectives and guidelines for code reviews is crucial for ensuring consistency and alignment across the team. Define the purpose of code reviews, whether it's to catch bugs, improve code readability, enforce coding standards, or share knowledge. Outline specific criteria for evaluating code, such as adherence to style guides, performance considerations, and error handling practices.

To set up guidelines for code reviews in a Git repository, teams can utilize tools like GitLab or GitHub to create a CONTRIBUTING.md file outlining the expectations and processes for code reviews. This document can detail criteria for code quality, review etiquette, and instructions for submitting and reviewing code changes.

Review Code in Small, Digestible Chunks: Breaking down code changes into smaller, manageable chunks facilitates more focused and thorough reviews. Large, monolithic changes can overwhelm reviewers and increase the likelihood of overlooking critical issues. Encourage developers to submit smaller, incremental changes that address specific features or bug fixes, allowing for more efficient and effective review processes.

In Git, developers can create feature branches for each individual task or issue they're working on, making it easier to review and merge changes incrementally. For example:

bashCopy code

```
git checkout -b feature/issue-123 # Make and commit changes git push origin feature/issue-123
```

Maintain a Positive and Constructive Atmosphere: Foster a culture of collaboration, respect, and constructive feedback during code reviews. Encourage reviewers to provide feedback in a courteous and respectful manner, focusing on improvement rather than criticism. Emphasize the importance of acknowledging and appreciating the efforts of fellow team members, even when suggesting changes or pointing out areas for improvement.

Establishing clear communication channels and guidelines for providing feedback can help maintain a positive atmosphere during code reviews. Encourage reviewers to focus on specific aspects of the code, provide actionable suggestions, and avoid personal attacks or derogatory comments.

Utilize Automated Tools and Linters: Leverage automated tools and linters to supplement manual code reviews and enforce coding standards consistently. Automated tools can help identify common issues such as syntax errors, style violations, and potential security vulnerabilities, allowing reviewers to focus on higher-level concerns. Integrate these tools into the continuous integration (CI) pipeline to ensure that code quality checks are performed automatically as part of the development workflow.

For example, teams can configure linters such as ESLint for JavaScript or Pylint for Python to run as pre-commit hooks or as part of CI/CD pipelines. This ensures that code changes adhere to coding standards and best practices before they are merged into the main codebase.

Encourage Active Participation and Knowledge Sharing: Promote active participation from all team members in the code review process to foster knowledge sharing and collective ownership of the codebase. Encourage developers to actively review code changes submitted by their peers, even if they are not directly involved in the project. By sharing insights, best practices, and lessons learned, team members can enhance their understanding of the codebase and contribute to its continuous improvement.

Consider implementing a rotation system where team members take turns serving as reviewers for code changes. This helps distribute the responsibility of code reviews evenly across the team and provides opportunities for developers to learn from each other's code.

Provide Timely and Actionable Feedback: Timely feedback is essential for maintaining momentum and ensuring that code changes are addressed promptly. Reviewers should strive to provide feedback in a timely manner, ideally within a reasonable timeframe that aligns with project deadlines and priorities. Additionally, feedback should be actionable, clearly articulating the rationale behind suggested changes and providing guidance on how to address identified issues.

Tools like GitHub or GitLab provide features for inline commenting and threaded discussions, enabling reviewers to provide specific feedback on individual lines of code. Encourage reviewers to be specific and provide context when suggesting changes or raising concerns, helping authors understand the reasoning behind the feedback.

Document Decisions and Learnings: Documenting decisions, learnings, and discussions arising from code reviews can provide valuable insights for future reference and help maintain institutional knowledge within the team. Consider keeping a record of significant discussions, decisions, and action items from code reviews in a centralized location, such as a shared document or wiki page. This documentation serves as a reference for team members and can help onboard new team members more effectively.

Additionally, consider holding periodic retrospective meetings to reflect on the effectiveness of the code review process and identify areas for improvement. Encourage open and honest discussions about what worked well, what could be improved, and any recurring issues or challenges encountered during code reviews.

By incorporating these best practices into their code review processes, software development teams can enhance collaboration, improve code quality, and accelerate the delivery of high-quality software products. Emphasizing clear communication, constructive feedback, and continuous improvement fosters a culture of excellence and drives success in software development endeavors.

Chapter 6: Effective Error Messaging

Effective error messaging is a cornerstone of user experience in software applications, offering users clear, concise, and actionable information when errors occur. Error messages serve as a crucial communication channel between the application and its users, helping them understand what went wrong and guiding them towards resolving the issue. To craft effective error messages, developers must adhere to several principles aimed at enhancing clarity, relevance, and usability.

Be Clear and Descriptive: Error messages should clearly communicate the nature of the problem encountered, using plain language that users can easily understand. Avoid using technical jargon or ambiguous terminology that may confuse users further. Instead, strive for clarity and specificity in describing the error situation, providing users with enough information to grasp the problem's cause and potential resolution.

For instance, when encountering a file not found error in a command-line interface (CLI) application, the error message should clearly state the missing file's name and location:

arduinoCopy code

Error: File 'example.txt' not found in directory '/path/to/directory'.

Provide Context and Guidance: In addition to describing the error, effective error messages should offer contextual information and guidance on how users can address the issue. This may include suggesting corrective actions, providing links to relevant documentation or support resources, or offering troubleshooting tips to help users resolve the error independently. By empowering users with actionable guidance, error messages can facilitate problem resolution and minimize frustration.

In a web application, an error message accompanying a network connectivity issue might provide guidance on troubleshooting steps, such as checking internet connectivity, refreshing the page, or contacting support:
vbnetCopy code

Network Error: Unable to establish a connection. Please check your internet connection and try again. If the issue persists, contact support for assistance.

Maintain Consistency and Standards: Consistency in error messaging fosters familiarity and predictability for users, enhancing their ability to interpret and respond to error conditions effectively. Follow established conventions and standards for error message formatting, tone, and presentation to ensure a cohesive user experience across the application. Consistent error messages reduce cognitive load on users, enabling them to navigate error situations more confidently.

CLI applications often adhere to consistent error message formats, such as prefixing error messages with a recognizable label like "Error:" and using consistent capitalization and punctuation:
bashCopy code

Error: Invalid command. Please check the command syntax and try again.

Offer Relevant Information: Tailor error messages to provide information that is relevant and meaningful to users in the context of their interactions with the application. Avoid overwhelming users with excessive technical details or irrelevant information that may obscure the core issue. Focus on delivering the most pertinent information necessary for users to understand the error and take appropriate action.

In a mobile app, an error message related to insufficient storage space should succinctly convey the problem and suggest actions users can take to free up space or manage storage:

sqlCopy code

Storage Full: Unable to complete action. Please delete unused files or apps to free up space and try again.

Empathize with Users: Effective error messaging acknowledges the user's experience and demonstrates empathy towards their frustration or inconvenience. Use a tone and phrasing that convey empathy and understanding of the user's situation, reassuring them that their concerns are recognized and taken seriously. Empathetic error messages can help mitigate user frustration and maintain positive perceptions of the application and brand.

In a desktop software application, an error message accompanying a critical error might express empathy and reassure users that the development team is aware of the issue and working to resolve it:

rustCopy code

Oops! Something went wrong. We apologize for the inconvenience. Our team has been notified of the problem, and we are working to fix it as soon as possible. Please try again later.

By adhering to these principles of effective error messaging, developers can enhance user understanding, facilitate problem resolution, and cultivate a positive user experience within their applications. Thoughtful and well-crafted error messages demonstrate a commitment to user-centric design and contribute to overall user satisfaction and retention.

Designing user-friendly error messages is a crucial aspect of creating intuitive and reliable software applications. Error messages serve as a means of communication between the application and its users, providing feedback when unexpected issues arise. To design user-friendly error messages, developers and designers must consider various factors, including clarity, relevance, and empathy towards the user's experience.

Understand the User Perspective: Before crafting error messages, it's essential to understand the user's perspective and anticipate their potential reactions to encountering errors. Users may experience frustration, confusion, or anxiety when confronted with error messages, especially if they hinder their progress or disrupt their workflow. By empathizing with users' emotions and mindset, designers can tailor error messages to address their concerns effectively.

For example, in a web application, encountering a server error can be frustrating for users, as it disrupts their browsing experience and prevents them from accessing desired content. In such cases, error messages should acknowledge the inconvenience caused to users and reassure them that the issue is being addressed.

Prioritize Clarity and Conciseness: Clear and concise error messages are essential for helping users understand the nature of the problem and take appropriate action. Avoid using technical jargon or ambiguous language that may confuse users further. Instead, use simple and straightforward language that conveys the error's cause and potential resolution.

In a command-line interface (CLI) application, clear error messages can help users diagnose and resolve issues more effectively. For instance, if a user attempts to execute a command with incorrect syntax, the CLI should provide a concise error message that highlights the error and suggests corrective actions:

bashCopy code

Error: Invalid command syntax. Please check the command format and try again.

Provide Actionable Guidance: Effective error messages should not only inform users about the error but also provide actionable guidance on how to resolve it. This may include suggesting specific steps users can take to address the issue, such as revising input data, adjusting settings, or contacting support for assistance. By offering actionable guidance, error messages empower users to navigate error situations more confidently.

In a mobile app, if a user encounters a network connection error while attempting to sync data, the error message should provide clear instructions on troubleshooting steps, such as checking network settings or restarting the device:

vbnetCopy code

Network Error: Unable to establish a connection. Please check your network settings and try again. If the issue persists, please restart your device.

Maintain Consistency and Familiarity: Consistency in error message design and formatting promotes familiarity and predictability for users, enabling them to recognize and interpret error messages more easily across different parts of the application. Establish standardized formats, layouts, and language conventions for error messages to create a cohesive user experience and reduce cognitive load on users.

Across web applications, consistency in error message design includes using similar color schemes, typography, and iconography to denote error severity and priority. Consistent error message placement and formatting also contribute to a seamless user experience.

Offer Additional Context When Necessary: In certain situations, providing additional context or information alongside the error message can help users better understand the underlying cause of the error and its potential implications. This may include displaying relevant error codes, stack traces, or links to further documentation or support resources to assist users in troubleshooting and problem resolution.

For example, in a desktop software application, if a user encounters a database connection error, the error message could include a brief explanation of the error code and suggest possible solutions:

vbnetCopy code

Database Connection Error (Error Code: 500): Unable to establish a connection to the database server. Please check your network connection and database settings. For further assistance, refer to the application documentation or contact support.

Test and Iterate: After designing error messages, it's essential to test them rigorously in real-world scenarios to ensure they effectively address users' needs and expectations. Conduct usability testing sessions to gather feedback from users about the clarity, relevance, and helpfulness of the error messages. Based on the feedback received, iterate on the design and content of the error messages to improve their effectiveness and user satisfaction.

Iterative testing and refinement of error messages help identify and address potential usability issues, ensuring that users can navigate error situations with confidence and ease.

By following these principles and best practices for designing user-friendly error messages, developers and designers can enhance the overall user experience of their applications and foster positive user interactions, even in the face of unexpected errors or disruptions. Effective error message design is integral to creating user-centric software experiences that prioritize clarity, empathy, and usability.

Chapter 7: Real-time Debugging Approaches

Real-time debugging tools and techniques play a pivotal role in software development, allowing developers to identify and resolve issues promptly during runtime. These tools provide insights into the application's behavior, performance, and execution flow in real-time, enabling developers to diagnose and debug problems effectively. By leveraging real-time debugging tools and techniques, developers can streamline the debugging process, improve software quality, and enhance the overall development workflow.

Debugging with Print Statements: One of the simplest yet effective real-time debugging techniques is using print statements to output variable values, function calls, or program flow information to the console or log files. In CLI applications, developers can insert print statements strategically throughout the code to track the program's execution and monitor the values of critical variables.

For example, in Python, developers can use the **print()** function to display variable values:

pythonCopy code

```
x = 10  print("The value of x is:", x)
```

Additionally, developers can use conditional print statements to selectively output information based on specific conditions, helping them narrow down the source of the issue.

Interactive Debuggers: Interactive debuggers are powerful tools that allow developers to inspect the state of a program, set breakpoints, and step through code execution in real-time. These debuggers provide a user-friendly interface for interacting with the code during runtime, enabling developers to identify logic errors, unexpected behavior, and performance bottlenecks.

In Python, the **pdb** module provides a built-in interactive debugger that developers can invoke from the command line:

Copy code

```
python -m pdb script.py
```

Once inside the debugger, developers can use commands like **break, step, next,** and **continue** to navigate through the code and inspect variable values at different stages of execution.

Logging Frameworks: Logging frameworks offer a systematic approach to capturing and analyzing application logs in real-time. By instrumenting the code with logging statements, developers can record important events, errors, and warnings during program execution. Logging frameworks provide flexibility in configuring log levels, output destinations, and message formats, making it easier to diagnose issues and monitor application health.

In Java, the **java.util.logging** framework provides a built-in logging mechanism that developers can use to log messages to various destinations:

javaCopy code

```
import java.util.logging.Logger; public class Example {
private static final Logger LOGGER =
Logger.getLogger(Example.class.getName()); public static
void main(String[] args) { LOGGER.info("Initializing
```

application...");   //   Application   logic
LOGGER.warning("Unexpected input received."); } }
Developers can configure the logging framework to output logs to the console, files, or external services, allowing for centralized log aggregation and analysis.

Remote Debugging: Remote debugging tools enable developers to debug applications running on remote servers or devices from their local development environment. This capability is particularly useful for troubleshooting issues in distributed systems, cloud-based applications, or IoT devices where direct access to the runtime environment may be limited.

In Java, developers can enable remote debugging by specifying the JVM debug port when starting the application:

bashCopy code

```
java -agentlib:jdwp=transport=dt_socket,server=y, suspend=n, address=*:8000 -jar app.jar
```

Once remote debugging is enabled, developers can connect their local debugger to the remote application using IDE-specific tools or command-line utilities, allowing them to debug code remotely with full access to debugging features.

Dynamic Code Analysis: Dynamic code analysis tools provide real-time insights into application behavior, performance, and resource utilization by monitoring code execution dynamically. These tools offer features such as memory profiling, code coverage analysis, and performance monitoring, enabling developers to identify memory leaks, performance bottlenecks, and other runtime issues.

In JavaScript, tools like Chrome DevTools offer dynamic code analysis capabilities for web applications. Developers can use the Performance and Memory tabs to analyze CPU usage, memory consumption, and network activity in real-time, helping them optimize application performance and diagnose runtime issues.

By incorporating these real-time debugging tools and techniques into their development workflow, developers can expedite the debugging process, reduce time-to-resolution for issues, and deliver higher-quality software products. Real-time debugging empowers developers to gain deeper insights into their code's behavior and performance, facilitating more efficient troubleshooting and problem resolution throughout the software development lifecycle.

Debugging in live environments presents unique challenges and considerations for developers, as it involves diagnosing and resolving issues in production systems without disrupting ongoing operations or affecting end users. While traditional debugging techniques are effective in development and testing environments, debugging in live environments requires a cautious and strategic approach to minimize risks and maintain system stability. By leveraging specialized tools, techniques, and best practices, developers can effectively debug live environments while ensuring minimal impact on system performance and user experience.

Logging and Monitoring: Logging and monitoring are fundamental aspects of debugging in live environments, as they provide real-time visibility into system behavior, performance metrics, and error occurrences. Developers can instrument their applications with comprehensive logging mechanisms to capture relevant information, including error messages, stack traces, and user interactions. Additionally, deploying monitoring solutions allows developers to track key performance indicators, detect anomalies, and receive alerts when issues arise.

In a Linux environment, developers can use the **tail** command to monitor log files in real-time:

bashCopy code

```
tail -f /var/log/application.log
```

By continuously monitoring logs and metrics, developers can quickly identify potential issues in live environments and take proactive measures to address them before they escalate.

Feature Flags and Rollbacks: Feature flags enable developers to toggle specific features or functionalities on or off in live environments, providing a controlled mechanism for debugging and testing in production. By using feature flags, developers can isolate problematic features, disable them temporarily, and observe the impact on system behavior without affecting the entire application. Furthermore, implementing rollback mechanisms allows developers to revert to a previous stable version of the application quickly in case of unexpected issues or regressions.

In a web application, developers can use feature flagging libraries like **LaunchDarkly** or **Flagsmith** to manage feature flags programmatically:

pythonCopy code

```
if feature_flag_enabled("new_feature"): # Execute new feature code else: # Execute fallback code
```

By judiciously using feature flags and rollbacks, developers can debug live environments with minimal disruption to users and maintain system reliability.

Remote Debugging and Diagnostics: Remote debugging tools and diagnostics enable developers to inspect and debug live applications remotely without directly accessing production servers or interrupting user activities. These tools allow developers to connect to live environments, analyze runtime data, and diagnose issues in real-time, all while minimizing downtime and system impact. Remote debugging solutions provide features such as code inspection, variable inspection, and breakpoint debugging, empowering developers to troubleshoot complex issues effectively.

In a Java application deployed on a remote server, developers can enable remote debugging by passing JVM arguments:

bashCopy code

```
java                                          -
agentlib:jdwp=transport=dt_socket,server=y, suspend =n,
address=*:5005 -jar app.jar
```

By connecting their local development environment to the remote server using an IDE like IntelliJ IDEA or Eclipse, developers can perform remote debugging seamlessly and gain insights into live system behavior.

Canary Deployments and A/B Testing: Canary deployments and A/B testing techniques allow developers to deploy changes to a subset of users or servers in live environments, enabling them to validate new features, configurations, or fixes before rolling them out to the entire user base. By gradually introducing changes and monitoring their impact, developers can identify potential issues early and mitigate risks associated with deploying changes directly to production. Additionally, A/B testing enables developers to compare the performance and user experience of different versions of the application in real-time.

In Kubernetes, developers can use canary deployment strategies with tools like Istio or Flagger to route traffic to new versions of microservices gradually:

```yaml
yamlCopy code
apiVersion: networking.istio.io/v1alpha3 kind: VirtualService metadata: name: my-app spec: hosts: - my-app.example.com http: - route: - destination: host: my-app subset: v1 weight: 90 timeout: 5s - route: - destination: host: my-app subset: v2 weight: 10 timeout: 5s
```

By leveraging canary deployments and A/B testing, developers can validate changes in live environments with reduced risk and gain valuable insights into their impact on system performance and user satisfaction.

Incident Response and Post-Mortem Analysis: Despite proactive measures, issues may still occur in live environments, necessitating swift incident response and post-mortem analysis. Establishing incident response procedures and conducting thorough post-incident reviews enable teams to identify root causes, assess impact, and implement preventive measures to mitigate similar issues in the future. Additionally, post-mortem analyses provide valuable learning opportunities for refining debugging processes, improving system resilience, and enhancing overall system reliability.

In a cloud environment, developers can use incident management platforms like PagerDuty or OpsGenie to coordinate incident response efforts and conduct post-incident reviews:

markdownCopy code

```
## Incident Summary - **Date:** [Date/Time] - **Duration:** [Duration] - **Impact:** [Affected users, services, etc.] ## Root Cause Analysis - [Root cause analysis findings] ## Corrective Actions - [Steps taken to resolve the incident] ## Lessons Learned - [Key takeaways and action items for future improvements]
```

By embracing a culture of continuous improvement and learning from incidents, development teams can enhance their ability to debug live environments effectively and maintain high levels of system availability and reliability.

Debugging in live environments requires a combination of proactive planning, strategic deployment practices, and effective incident response procedures. By employing logging and monitoring solutions, leveraging feature flags and rollbacks, utilizing remote debugging tools, implementing canary deployments and A/B testing, and conducting thorough incident response and post-mortem analyses, developers can debug live environments with confidence while minimizing disruption and maximizing system resilience.

Chapter 8: Utilizing Debugging Symbols

Understanding debugging symbols is crucial for effective debugging in software development, as they provide essential metadata and mapping information that aids in translating compiled code back to its original source form. Debugging symbols, also known as debug information or debug data, contain mappings between machine code instructions and corresponding source code constructs such as variables, functions, and line numbers. These symbols facilitate various debugging tasks, including setting breakpoints, inspecting variables, and analyzing stack traces, by enabling developers to correlate machine code behavior with source code logic seamlessly.

Debugging symbols are generated during the compilation process and are typically stored in separate files or embedded within executable binaries alongside the compiled code. These symbols contain metadata that maps machine-level instructions to source code elements, allowing debugging tools to reconstruct the original source context during debugging sessions. Common formats for debugging symbols include Program Database (PDB) files on Windows, Debugging Information Format (DWARF) on Unix-based systems, and Breakpad symbols for cross-platform compatibility.

In a Unix-based environment, developers can generate debugging symbols using the **-g** flag with GCC or Clang compilers:

bashCopy code

```
gcc -g -o my_program my_program.c
```

This command instructs the compiler to include debugging information in the generated executable file **my_program**, facilitating subsequent debugging sessions.

Debugging symbols consist of various types of information, including:

Symbol Tables: Symbol tables contain mappings between symbols (such as function names, variable names, and type definitions) and memory addresses or offsets within the executable. These tables enable debuggers to associate machine instructions with corresponding source code entities during debugging sessions, facilitating symbol resolution and source-level debugging.

Line Number Information: Line number information maps memory addresses or offsets within the executable to corresponding source code line numbers. This information allows debuggers to display source code alongside machine code instructions during debugging sessions, enabling developers to correlate program behavior with specific source code lines accurately.

Type Information: Type information describes the data types of variables, function parameters, and return values within the program. This metadata enables debuggers to interpret memory contents correctly during variable inspection and expression evaluation, facilitating accurate debugging and runtime analysis.

Debugging symbols play a crucial role in various debugging scenarios, including:

Setting Breakpoints: Debugging symbols enable developers to set breakpoints at specific source code lines or function entry points during debugging sessions. By leveraging symbol information, debuggers can accurately identify corresponding memory addresses or offsets within the executable, allowing breakpoints to be set precisely at desired locations within the source code.

Variable Inspection: During debugging sessions, developers often need to inspect the values of variables and data structures within the program. Debugging symbols provide type information and memory location mappings for variables, enabling debuggers to display variable values accurately and facilitate runtime analysis and troubleshooting.

Stack Trace Analysis: When diagnosing runtime errors or exceptions, stack traces provide valuable information about the sequence of function calls leading to the error. Debugging symbols enhance stack trace readability by associating memory addresses or offsets within the executable with corresponding source code functions and file paths, enabling developers to identify the origins of errors quickly and pinpoint problematic code sections for resolution.

Executable Analysis and Reverse Engineering: Debugging symbols are invaluable for analyzing executable binaries and conducting reverse engineering tasks. Reverse engineers and security analysts use debugging symbols to reconstruct the original source code structure, identify program functionalities, and analyze program behavior systematically. Additionally, debugging symbols aid in vulnerability research, malware analysis, and software auditing by providing insights into program internals and facilitating code comprehension.

While debugging symbols offer significant benefits for software development and debugging, developers should be mindful of potential drawbacks, including increased executable size and potential information leakage in release builds. To mitigate these concerns, developers can utilize separate debug builds or strip debugging symbols from release binaries using tools like **strip** on Unix-based systems:

bashCopy code

strip --strip-debug my_program

This command removes debugging symbols from the executable **my_program**, reducing its size and minimizing information disclosure risks in production environments.

In summary, understanding debugging symbols is essential for proficient software debugging and analysis. By providing critical metadata and mapping information, debugging symbols enable developers to correlate machine code behavior with source code logic accurately, facilitating breakpoint setting, variable inspection, stack trace analysis, and executable analysis tasks. While debugging symbols offer numerous benefits for software development and debugging, developers should be mindful of associated trade-offs and employ best practices to optimize their usage in various debugging scenarios.

Incorporating debugging symbols into the debugging process is essential for efficient and effective troubleshooting in software development. Debugging symbols, which contain metadata and mapping information linking machine code instructions to corresponding source code constructs, play a crucial role in enhancing debugging capabilities and streamlining the identification and resolution of software defects. By leveraging debugging symbols, developers can gain valuable insights into program behavior, facilitate source-level debugging, and expedite the diagnosis and correction of bugs.

To incorporate debugging symbols into the debugging process, developers must ensure that these symbols are generated and made available during the compilation of the software. This typically involves compiling the code with debugging information enabled using compiler flags such as **-g** in GCC or Clang. For example, when compiling a C or C++ program with GCC, developers can include debugging symbols using the following command:

bashCopy code

```
gcc -g -o my_program my_program.c
```

This command instructs the GCC compiler to generate debugging symbols and include them in the executable file **my_program**, enabling subsequent debugging sessions.

Once the software is compiled with debugging symbols, developers can utilize various debugging tools and techniques to analyze and troubleshoot issues effectively. Debugging symbols facilitate several key aspects of the debugging process, including:

Symbol Resolution: Debugging symbols enable debuggers to correlate machine code instructions with corresponding source code constructs, such as function names, variable names, and line numbers. This allows developers to navigate and inspect the codebase at the source level during debugging sessions, facilitating precise identification of program elements and their relationships.

Breakpoint Setting: Debugging symbols streamline the process of setting breakpoints at specific source code locations during debugging sessions. By associating machine code addresses with source code lines, debugging tools can accurately identify breakpoints and halt program execution at desired locations, enabling developers to examine program state and behavior systematically.

Variable Inspection: During debugging sessions, developers often need to inspect the values of variables and data structures within the program. Debugging symbols provide type information and memory location mappings for variables, allowing debuggers to display variable values accurately and facilitate runtime analysis and troubleshooting.

Stack Trace Analysis: Stack traces provide valuable information about the sequence of function calls leading to an error or exception. Debugging symbols enhance stack trace readability by associating memory addresses with corresponding source code functions and file paths, enabling developers to trace the execution flow and identify the origins of errors quickly.

In addition to traditional debugging tools, incorporating debugging symbols into the debugging process can also benefit from advanced debugging techniques and practices. For example, symbolic debuggers such as GDB (GNU Debugger) offer powerful features for source-level debugging, stack trace analysis, and variable inspection, leveraging debugging symbols to provide comprehensive debugging capabilities.

Moreover, developers can utilize integrated development environments (IDEs) that offer seamless integration with debugging symbols and provide intuitive debugging workflows. IDEs such as Visual Studio Code, IntelliJ IDEA, and Eclipse offer robust debugging features, including symbol navigation, breakpoint management, and variable inspection, making it easier for developers to debug their code efficiently.

Furthermore, leveraging debugging symbols in conjunction with other debugging aids, such as logging and runtime instrumentation, can enhance the effectiveness of the debugging process. By combining multiple debugging techniques and tools, developers can gain deeper insights into program behavior, diagnose complex issues more effectively, and expedite the resolution of software defects.

Incorporating debugging symbols into the debugging process is essential for modern software development practices, where rapid iteration and continuous integration are paramount. By enabling source-level debugging, precise breakpoint setting, and comprehensive variable inspection, debugging symbols empower developers to diagnose and rectify bugs efficiently, ultimately improving software quality and reliability.

Chapter 9: Network Protocol Analysis

Network protocol analysis is a fundamental aspect of network troubleshooting and security analysis in modern computer networks. It involves the examination and interpretation of network traffic to understand the communication protocols used between devices and systems. By analyzing network packets, headers, and payloads, network administrators and security professionals can gain insights into network behavior, identify anomalies, diagnose performance issues, and detect security threats.

Wireshark, a popular open-source network protocol analyzer, provides powerful capabilities for capturing, analyzing, and dissecting network traffic in real-time. To capture network traffic using Wireshark, users can start a packet capture session on a network interface using the following command:

bashCopy code

wireshark -i eth0

This command instructs Wireshark to start capturing network traffic on the Ethernet interface **eth0**. Once the packet capture session is active, Wireshark displays a live stream of captured packets, allowing users to inspect and analyze network communication in real-time.

Network protocol analysis involves several key concepts and techniques:

Packet Capture: The first step in network protocol analysis is capturing network packets. This process involves intercepting and recording network traffic passing through a network interface. Packet capture tools like Wireshark capture packets at the data link layer (Layer 2) or network layer (Layer 3) of the OSI model, allowing users to analyze traffic at different levels of the network stack.

Protocol Dissection: Once packets are captured, they can be dissected and analyzed to understand the protocols used in network communication. Protocol dissection involves parsing packet headers and payloads to extract protocol-specific information such as source and destination addresses, port numbers, protocol flags, and data payloads. Wireshark provides built-in dissectors for a wide range of network protocols, allowing users to view protocol details and decode packet contents.

Traffic Filtering: Network protocol analyzers often support traffic filtering capabilities, allowing users to focus on specific types of network traffic or communication patterns. Filters can be based on various criteria such as source and destination addresses, port numbers, protocol types, and packet contents. By applying filters, users can isolate relevant traffic and reduce the volume of data to analyze.

Session Reconstruction: In network protocol analysis, it is often essential to reconstruct higher-level sessions or conversations from captured packets. Session reconstruction involves identifying related packets exchanged between network hosts and assembling them into coherent sessions or transactions. This process enables users to analyze application-layer protocols such as HTTP, FTP, and DNS and understand the flow of data between client and server systems.

Anomaly Detection: Network protocol analysis also plays a crucial role in detecting anomalies and identifying potential security threats within network traffic. By analyzing traffic patterns, packet headers, and payload contents, analysts can identify suspicious behavior such as port scanning, network reconnaissance, malware infections, and data exfiltration attempts. Anomaly detection techniques may involve statistical analysis, signature-based detection, and machine learning algorithms to identify abnormal network behavior.

Performance Monitoring: In addition to security analysis, network protocol analysis is valuable for monitoring network performance and diagnosing connectivity issues. By analyzing network traffic patterns, packet loss rates, latency metrics, and throughput statistics, administrators can identify bottlenecks, troubleshoot connectivity problems, and optimize network configurations to improve performance.

Overall, network protocol analysis is a fundamental skill for network administrators, security analysts, and IT professionals responsible for managing and securing computer networks. By mastering the basics of packet capture, protocol dissection, traffic filtering, session reconstruction, anomaly detection, and performance monitoring, practitioners can effectively analyze network traffic, diagnose issues, and mitigate security risks in modern networks.

Network protocol analysis tools and methods are essential components of modern network administration and security practices, providing insights into network communication, troubleshooting connectivity issues, and detecting security threats. These tools offer comprehensive capabilities for capturing, analyzing, and interpreting network traffic, enabling administrators and security professionals to gain a deep understanding of network behavior and ensure the integrity and security of their network infrastructure.

Wireshark, one of the most widely used open-source network protocol analyzers, offers a rich set of features for capturing and dissecting network packets. To capture network traffic using Wireshark, users can initiate a packet capture session on a specific network interface using the **tshark** command-line tool, which is part of the Wireshark suite:

bashCopy code

```
tshark -i eth0 -w capture.pcap
```

This command instructs tshark to capture network traffic on the Ethernet interface **eth0** and save the captured packets to a file named **capture.pcap**. Once the packet capture session is complete, users can analyze the captured packets using Wireshark's graphical user interface (GUI) or other command-line tools.

In addition to Wireshark, several other network protocol analysis tools offer specialized functionalities and capabilities for different use cases. Tcpdump, a command-line packet analyzer similar to tshark, is commonly used for capturing and displaying network packets in real-time. To capture packets with tcpdump, users can execute the following command:

bashCopy code

```
tcpdump -i eth0 -w capture.pcap
```

This command captures network traffic on the Ethernet interface **eth0** and writes the captured packets to a file named **capture.pcap**.

Apart from packet capture tools, network protocol analyzers often incorporate advanced analysis and visualization features to facilitate in-depth analysis of network traffic. Tools like NetworkMiner, a network forensic analysis tool, provide capabilities for extracting files, emails, and other artifacts from captured network traffic, enabling digital forensics investigations and incident response activities.

Furthermore, intrusion detection and prevention systems (IDS/IPS) leverage network protocol analysis techniques to detect and prevent malicious activities on the network. Snort, an open-source network intrusion detection system (NIDS), utilizes a combination of signature-based detection and protocol analysis to identify and block network-based attacks in real-time.

When conducting network protocol analysis, practitioners employ various methods and techniques to extract valuable insights from captured network traffic. These methods include:

Protocol Dissection: Analyzing packet headers and payloads to understand the communication protocols used in network traffic. This involves decoding protocol-specific information such as source and destination addresses, port numbers, protocol flags, and data payloads.

Traffic Filtering: Filtering network traffic based on specific criteria such as source and destination addresses, port numbers, protocol types, and packet contents. This allows analysts to focus on relevant traffic and reduce the volume of data to analyze.

Session Reconstruction: Reconstructing higher-level sessions or conversations from captured packets to analyze application-layer protocols such as HTTP, FTP, and DNS. This enables analysts to understand the flow of data between client and server systems and identify potential security issues.

Anomaly Detection: Identifying abnormal patterns and behaviors within network traffic that may indicate security threats or performance issues. Anomaly detection techniques leverage statistical analysis, machine learning algorithms, and signature-based detection to detect suspicious activity.

Performance Monitoring: Monitoring network performance metrics such as packet loss rates, latency, and throughput to diagnose connectivity issues and optimize network configurations for better performance.

By leveraging network protocol analysis tools and methods, organizations can enhance their network security posture, troubleshoot connectivity issues, and optimize network performance effectively. These tools provide valuable insights into network traffic behavior and enable proactive monitoring and management of network infrastructure to ensure its reliability, availability, and security.

Chapter 10: Advanced Error Localization Strategies

Advanced error localization techniques are indispensable for software developers and system administrators striving to identify and resolve complex software defects efficiently. These techniques encompass a variety of approaches and methodologies aimed at pinpointing the root causes of elusive errors and anomalies in software systems. Leveraging sophisticated tools and methodologies, practitioners can gain deeper insights into the underlying causes of software failures, streamline the debugging process, and expedite the resolution of critical issues.

One prominent approach to advanced error localization involves the utilization of dynamic analysis tools, such as Valgrind, a powerful instrumentation framework for building dynamic analysis tools. Valgrind offers a suite of tools, including Memcheck, AddressSanitizer, and ThreadSanitizer, which enable developers to detect memory leaks, buffer overflows, and threading issues in their applications. To analyze a program with Valgrind's Memcheck tool, developers can execute the following command:

bashCopy code

```
valgrind --tool=memcheck ./my_program
```

This command runs the specified program under the Memcheck tool's supervision, allowing it to detect memory-related errors and provide detailed diagnostic information to aid in debugging.

Another advanced error localization technique involves the use of symbolic execution, a sophisticated program analysis technique that explores different execution paths through a program symbolically to identify potential vulnerabilities and errors. Symbolic execution tools, such as KLEE and S2E, automatically generate test cases that exercise various program paths, allowing developers to uncover hidden bugs and security vulnerabilities. To perform symbolic execution with KLEE, developers can use the following command:

bashCopy code

```
klee --libc=uclibc ./my_program
```

This command instructs KLEE to symbolically execute the specified program, leveraging the uclibc library for compatibility with KLEE's symbolic execution engine.

In addition to dynamic analysis and symbolic execution, fault injection techniques play a crucial role in advanced error localization. Fault injection involves deliberately introducing faults or errors into a software system to observe its behavior under abnormal conditions and assess its resilience. Fault injection tools, such as Jinx and Chaos Monkey, enable developers to simulate various failure scenarios, including network errors, disk failures, and hardware faults, to validate the robustness and fault tolerance of their applications. To inject faults into a running system using Chaos Monkey, operators can execute the following command:

bashCopy code

```
chaosmonkey inject network-exception
```

This command instructs Chaos Monkey to inject network exceptions into the target system, causing network-related errors and disruptions.

Furthermore, advanced error localization techniques often incorporate machine learning and data mining algorithms to analyze large volumes of software execution traces, logs, and telemetry data to identify patterns and anomalies indicative of potential errors or performance issues. Machine learning frameworks, such as TensorFlow and scikit-learn, enable practitioners to build predictive models that can classify and predict software defects based on historical data. To train a machine learning model using TensorFlow, data scientists can use the following Python code:

```python
pythonCopy code
import tensorflow as tf from tensorflow.keras import layers # Define and compile the model model = tf.keras.Sequential([ layers.Dense(64, activation='relu'), layers.Dense(64, activation='relu'), layers.Dense(1, activation='sigmoid') ])
model.compile(optimizer='adam', loss='binary_crossentropy', metrics=['accuracy']) # Train the model model.fit(X_train, y_train, epochs=10, batch_size=32, validation_data=(X_val, y_val))
```

This code snippet defines a simple neural network model using TensorFlow's Keras API and trains it on labeled data to classify software defects.

By embracing advanced error localization techniques and leveraging cutting-edge tools and methodologies, software development teams can enhance their ability to identify and address software defects effectively, ultimately improving the quality, reliability, and security of their software products.

Error localization is a critical aspect of software development and debugging, and case studies provide valuable insights into real-world scenarios where effective error localization techniques have been applied to diagnose and resolve challenging software defects. By examining these case studies, developers can gain a deeper understanding of the practical applications of error localization techniques and learn from the experiences of others in the field.

One notable case study involves a large e-commerce platform experiencing intermittent errors in its checkout process, leading to lost revenue and frustrated customers. To diagnose the root cause of these errors, the development team utilized log analysis tools, such as Splunk and ELK Stack, to analyze the application logs and identify patterns associated with failed checkout transactions. By correlating error messages with user interactions and system events, they were able to pinpoint a bug in the payment processing module that caused occasional timeouts under high load conditions. To mitigate the issue, they implemented performance improvements and error handling mechanisms, effectively resolving the intermittent errors and improving the reliability of the checkout process.

In another case study, a software-as-a-service (SaaS) company encountered performance degradation and frequent crashes in its web application during peak usage periods. To address these issues, the engineering team employed a combination of profiling tools, such as Java Flight Recorder and YourKit, to identify performance bottlenecks and memory leaks contributing to the instability of the application. By analyzing heap dumps and thread dumps generated by these tools, they uncovered inefficiencies in the application's database access layer and inefficient memory usage patterns. Armed with this information, they optimized database queries, implemented caching strategies, and optimized memory allocation, resulting in significant performance improvements and enhanced system stability.

Additionally, case studies in error localization often highlight the importance of collaboration and knowledge sharing within development teams. In one instance, a software development company encountered a critical security vulnerability in its web application that exposed sensitive customer data to unauthorized access. To remediate the vulnerability, the security team conducted a thorough code review and penetration testing, leveraging tools like OWASP ZAP and Burp Suite to identify and exploit security weaknesses in the application. Through collaboration between the development, security, and operations teams, they were able to patch the vulnerability, update access controls, and implement additional security measures to prevent similar exploits in the future.

Furthermore, case studies illustrate the effectiveness of proactive monitoring and incident response strategies in detecting and mitigating software defects before they escalate into production issues. For example, a financial services firm implemented a comprehensive monitoring solution using tools like Prometheus and Grafana to track application performance metrics and alert on abnormal behavior. When anomalies were detected, an incident response team would be immediately notified, enabling them to investigate and address potential issues before they impacted end users. By proactively monitoring their systems and responding swiftly to incidents, the company was able to maintain high availability and reliability for their critical financial applications.

Overall, case studies in error localization offer valuable lessons and best practices for software developers and engineers seeking to improve their debugging skills and enhance the quality and reliability of their software systems. By analyzing real-world scenarios and learning from the experiences of others, development teams can better understand the challenges associated with error localization and apply effective strategies to diagnose and resolve software defects efficiently.

BOOK 4
DEBUGGING PLAYBOOK
EXPERT APPROACHES TO COMPREHENSIVE SYSTEM
TESTING AND SECURITY

ROB BOTWRIGHT

Chapter 1: Advanced System Testing Methodologies

Advanced testing approaches encompass a range of sophisticated techniques and methodologies designed to uncover complex software defects and ensure the reliability, performance, and security of software systems. These approaches go beyond traditional testing methods to address the evolving challenges of modern software development, including increasing complexity, rapid release cycles, and the need for robust security measures. Next, we will explore several advanced testing approaches and examine how they can be applied to enhance the quality of software products.

One advanced testing approach is mutation testing, a technique that involves introducing small modifications, or "mutations," to the source code and then running the test suite to determine if the tests can detect these mutations. The idea behind mutation testing is to evaluate the effectiveness of the test suite by measuring its ability to detect changes in the code that could potentially introduce bugs. Tools like PITest and Stryker can automate the process of generating mutations and analyzing test coverage, allowing developers to identify weak spots in their test suites and improve overall test effectiveness.

Another advanced testing approach is property-based testing, which focuses on specifying the properties or invariants that the software should adhere to, rather than writing specific test cases. Property-based testing frameworks like QuickCheck and Hypothesis use random input generation to systematically explore the behavior of the software and verify that it satisfies the specified properties across a wide range of inputs. By defining concise and expressive properties, developers can uncover edge cases and corner cases that may not be covered by traditional test cases, leading to more comprehensive test coverage and higher confidence in the correctness of the software.

Furthermore, chaos engineering has emerged as a powerful technique for testing the resilience and fault tolerance of distributed systems. Inspired by the principles of chaos theory, chaos engineering involves deliberately injecting faults and failures into a system in order to observe how it behaves under adverse conditions. Tools like Chaos Monkey and Gremlin allow engineers to simulate real-world outages and infrastructure failures, enabling them to identify weaknesses in their systems and implement proactive measures to improve reliability and recoverability.

Additionally, security testing is an essential component of advanced testing approaches, especially in the context of modern web applications and cloud-native architectures. Techniques such as penetration testing, security scanning, and threat modeling can help identify vulnerabilities and security risks in software systems, allowing organizations to mitigate potential threats and protect sensitive data. Tools like OWASP ZAP, Nessus, and Burp Suite provide automated scanning and analysis capabilities, enabling security teams to identify and remediate security vulnerabilities before they can be exploited by malicious actors.

Moreover, performance testing is crucial for ensuring the scalability and responsiveness of software systems under varying loads and conditions. Advanced performance testing techniques, such as stress testing, endurance testing, and spike testing, help assess the robustness and scalability of applications by subjecting them to extreme conditions and measuring their performance metrics. Tools like Apache JMeter, Gatling, and Locust enable engineers to simulate realistic user behavior and analyze system performance under different scenarios, allowing them to optimize resource utilization and improve overall system responsiveness.

In summary, advanced testing approaches offer valuable techniques and methodologies for ensuring the quality, reliability, and security of software systems in today's fast-paced and increasingly complex development environments. By leveraging techniques such as mutation testing, property-based testing, chaos engineering, security testing, and performance testing, organizations can identify and address potential issues early in the development lifecycle, ultimately delivering higher-quality software products that meet the evolving needs of users and stakeholders.

Innovative testing methodologies represent a paradigm shift in how software testing is approached, leveraging cutting-edge techniques and technologies to address the challenges of modern software development. These methodologies go beyond traditional testing approaches to provide more efficient, effective, and comprehensive ways of ensuring the quality and reliability of software systems. Next, we will explore several innovative testing methodologies and examine how they can be applied to improve the software development process.

One innovative testing methodology is model-based testing, which involves creating formal models of the system under test and then automatically generating test cases from these models. Model-based testing allows for systematic exploration of the system's behavior and can uncover complex interaction scenarios that may be difficult to identify using traditional testing methods. Tools like Spec Explorer and TorX enable engineers to specify system behavior using formal models, automatically generate test cases, and systematically verify system properties, leading to more thorough test coverage and higher confidence in the correctness of the software.

Another innovative testing methodology is crowdtesting, which harnesses the power of crowdsourcing to perform testing activities across a diverse and distributed group of testers. Crowdtesting platforms like Applause and Testbirds allow organizations to crowdsource testing tasks to a global community of testers, who can provide feedback, report bugs, and perform usability testing on a wide range of devices and platforms. By tapping into the collective knowledge and expertise of a large pool of testers, crowdtesting enables organizations to quickly identify issues, gather real-world feedback, and ensure the quality of their software products across various environments and use cases.

Furthermore, AI-driven testing is emerging as a transformative approach to software testing, leveraging machine learning and artificial intelligence techniques to automate testing tasks, generate test cases, and analyze test results. AI-powered testing tools like Test.ai and Applitools use machine learning algorithms to automatically generate test scripts, identify UI elements, and detect visual defects, allowing for faster test execution and more accurate defect detection. By leveraging the power of AI, organizations can streamline their testing processes, improve test coverage, and accelerate the delivery of high-quality software products to market.

Moreover, chaos engineering has gained traction as a novel testing methodology for evaluating the resilience and reliability of distributed systems. Inspired by the principles of chaos theory, chaos engineering involves deliberately injecting faults and failures into a system in order to observe how it behaves under adverse conditions. Tools like Chaos Monkey and Gremlin enable engineers to simulate real-world outages and infrastructure failures, allowing them to identify weaknesses in their systems and implement proactive measures to improve resilience and recoverability.

Additionally, blockchain testing has emerged as a specialized testing discipline for validating the functionality, performance, and security of blockchain-based applications and smart contracts. Blockchain testing tools like Truffle and Ganache provide developers with frameworks for writing and executing automated tests for smart contracts, verifying consensus algorithms, and simulating network conditions. By conducting thorough testing of blockchain applications, organizations can ensure the integrity and reliability of their decentralized systems and mitigate potential security risks.

In summary, innovative testing methodologies offer novel approaches and techniques for ensuring the quality, reliability, and security of software systems in today's fast-paced and dynamic development landscape. By embracing methodologies such as model-based testing, crowdtesting, AI-driven testing, chaos engineering, and blockchain testing, organizations can enhance their testing practices, accelerate their software delivery cycles, and deliver higher-quality products that meet the evolving needs of users and stakeholders.

Chapter 2: Security Testing Fundamentals

Introduction to security testing is crucial in today's software development landscape, where the proliferation of cyber threats poses significant risks to organizations and their digital assets. Security testing encompasses a range of techniques and methodologies aimed at identifying vulnerabilities, weaknesses, and security flaws in software applications, networks, and systems. This chapter explores the fundamentals of security testing and provides insights into its importance, key concepts, and best practices.

Security testing is essential for ensuring the confidentiality, integrity, and availability of information assets, protecting against unauthorized access, data breaches, and cyber attacks. By systematically evaluating the security posture of software systems, organizations can mitigate security risks, comply with regulatory requirements, and safeguard sensitive data from exploitation. Security testing is an integral part of the software development lifecycle (SDLC), encompassing activities such as threat modeling, security architecture review, penetration testing, and code analysis.

One of the primary objectives of security testing is to identify and mitigate vulnerabilities that could be exploited by malicious actors to compromise the security of a system. Vulnerability assessment is a key component of security testing, involving the identification, classification, and prioritization of security weaknesses in software applications and infrastructure. Vulnerability scanning tools such as Nessus, OpenVAS, and Qualys provide automated capabilities for scanning systems and networks for known vulnerabilities, misconfigurations, and security issues.

Penetration testing, also known as ethical hacking, is another critical aspect of security testing, focusing on simulating real-world attacks to assess the resilience of a system's defenses. Penetration testers use a variety of techniques and tools to exploit vulnerabilities, gain unauthorized access, and escalate privileges within a target environment. Tools like Metasploit, Burp Suite, and Nmap are commonly used by penetration testers to identify and exploit security weaknesses in web applications, networks, and infrastructure.

In addition to vulnerability assessment and penetration testing, security testing also encompasses activities such as security code review, security architecture review, and security-focused testing techniques such as fuzz testing and security regression testing. Security code review involves examining the source code of an application to identify potential security vulnerabilities, coding errors, and insecure coding practices. Automated static code analysis tools like Checkmarx and Fortify can assist in identifying security issues in source code.

Furthermore, security architecture review evaluates the overall security design of a system, including its network topology, access control mechanisms, encryption protocols, and data protection measures. By analyzing the architecture of a system from a security perspective, organizations can identify design flaws, misconfigurations, and vulnerabilities that may expose the system to security risks.

Moreover, security testing also encompasses specialized testing techniques such as fuzz testing, which involves sending malformed or unexpected input to a software application to identify potential security vulnerabilities and stability issues. Fuzzing tools like American Fuzzy Lop (AFL) and Peach Fuzzer automate the process of generating and sending fuzzed input to target applications, helping to uncover vulnerabilities such as buffer overflows, format string vulnerabilities, and input validation errors.

Additionally, security regression testing focuses on verifying that security controls and mitigations implemented to address previously identified vulnerabilities remain effective over time. By conducting regular regression tests, organizations can ensure that security patches, configuration changes, and updates do not introduce new security vulnerabilities or regressions into the system.

In summary, security testing is a critical aspect of modern software development, essential for identifying and mitigating security risks, protecting sensitive data, and maintaining the trust and confidence of users. By integrating security testing into the software development lifecycle and adopting a proactive approach to security, organizations can enhance the resilience of their systems, reduce the likelihood of security breaches, and mitigate the impact of cyber threats.

Core principles of security testing form the foundation of effective cybersecurity practices, guiding organizations in identifying, assessing, and mitigating security risks across their digital assets and infrastructures. These principles encompass fundamental concepts and methodologies essential for ensuring the confidentiality, integrity, and availability of information systems, as well as protecting against unauthorized access, data breaches, and cyber threats.

One of the primary principles of security testing is comprehensiveness, which emphasizes the importance of conducting thorough and comprehensive assessments of the entire attack surface of an organization's IT environment. This includes not only applications and systems but also network infrastructure, databases, and cloud services. To achieve comprehensiveness in security testing, organizations employ a variety of techniques and tools tailored to the specific characteristics of each component of their IT infrastructure.

Another key principle is risk-based prioritization, which involves identifying and prioritizing security risks based on their potential impact on the organization's business objectives and assets. This principle recognizes that not all security risks are created equal and that limited resources should be allocated to address the most critical and high-impact vulnerabilities first. Risk-based prioritization enables organizations to focus their security testing efforts on areas that pose the greatest threat to their operations and sensitive data.

Additionally, security testing should be conducted using a combination of automated and manual techniques to achieve both breadth and depth in vulnerability assessment. Automated scanning tools such as vulnerability scanners and web application scanners can efficiently identify common security issues and misconfigurations across large-scale IT environments.

However, manual testing by experienced security professionals is essential for uncovering more complex and sophisticated vulnerabilities that may evade automated detection.

Moreover, security testing should be conducted in a controlled and isolated environment to minimize the risk of disrupting critical business operations or inadvertently causing damage to production systems. This principle of isolation involves setting up dedicated test environments or sandboxes where security testing can be performed safely without impacting the organization's live systems or data. By isolating testing activities, organizations can mitigate the risk of unintended consequences and ensure the integrity and availability of their production environments.

Furthermore, security testing should adhere to established industry standards and best practices to ensure consistency, reliability, and accuracy in the assessment of security controls and vulnerabilities. Adherence to standards such as the Open Web Application Security Project (OWASP) Top 10, the Common Vulnerability Scoring System (CVSS), and the National Institute of Standards and Technology (NIST) Special Publication 800-53 helps organizations benchmark their security posture against recognized benchmarks and frameworks.

In addition to technical assessments, security testing should also include considerations of human factors and organizational processes that may impact the security of IT systems. This principle recognizes that security is not solely a technical problem but also a socio-technical one, influenced by factors such as user behavior, organizational culture, and governance practices. Security awareness training, user education, and policy enforcement are essential components of a holistic security testing program.

Moreover, security testing should be conducted periodically and continuously throughout the software development lifecycle (SDLC), from initial design and development stages to deployment and maintenance phases. This principle of continuous testing ensures that security vulnerabilities are identified and addressed proactively, rather than waiting until they are discovered by malicious actors or during post-production audits. By integrating security testing into the SDLC, organizations can reduce the risk of security incidents and minimize the cost and effort required to remediate vulnerabilities.

Additionally, security testing should be conducted with the mindset of an attacker, leveraging techniques and methodologies that mimic real-world threats and attack scenarios. This principle of adversarial testing involves thinking like a hacker, identifying potential attack vectors, and assessing the resilience of security controls from an adversary's perspective. By adopting an adversarial mindset, organizations can uncover hidden vulnerabilities and weaknesses that may not be apparent through traditional security testing approaches.

Furthermore, security testing should be conducted transparently and collaboratively across different teams and stakeholders within an organization. This principle of transparency promotes open communication, knowledge sharing, and collaboration among security professionals, developers, operations teams, and business stakeholders. By fostering a culture of collaboration and shared responsibility for security, organizations can leverage the collective expertise and insights of their teams to identify and address security risks effectively.

In summary, core principles of security testing provide a framework for organizations to establish robust and effective cybersecurity practices, enabling them to identify, assess, and mitigate security risks across their digital infrastructure. By embracing principles such as comprehensiveness, risk-based prioritization, automation, isolation, adherence to standards, consideration of human factors, continuous testing, adversarial mindset, and transparency, organizations can strengthen their security posture and better defend against evolving cyber threats.

Chapter 3: Penetration Testing Techniques

Penetration testing, often referred to as pen testing, is a proactive cybersecurity practice aimed at identifying and assessing security vulnerabilities within an organization's IT infrastructure, applications, and network systems. It involves simulating real-world cyber attacks to evaluate the effectiveness of existing security controls and measures, as well as to uncover potential weaknesses that could be exploited by malicious actors. Penetration testing plays a crucial role in helping organizations proactively identify and address security vulnerabilities before they can be exploited by attackers, thereby reducing the risk of data breaches, financial losses, and reputational damage.

One of the key objectives of penetration testing is to identify vulnerabilities and security weaknesses that may exist within an organization's IT infrastructure and systems. This includes vulnerabilities in network devices, servers, databases, web applications, and other critical components of the IT environment. Penetration testers employ a variety of tools and techniques to systematically identify and exploit security vulnerabilities, ranging from automated vulnerability scanners to manual techniques such as network reconnaissance, port scanning, and service enumeration. By uncovering vulnerabilities, organizations can prioritize remediation efforts and strengthen their overall security posture.

Moreover, penetration testing provides valuable insights into the potential impact of security vulnerabilities on an organization's operations and sensitive data. By simulating real-world attack scenarios, penetration testers can assess the severity and likelihood of exploitation for each identified vulnerability, as well as the potential consequences of a successful attack. This enables organizations to make informed decisions about risk mitigation strategies and resource allocation, ensuring that limited resources are directed towards addressing the most critical security risks.

Furthermore, penetration testing helps organizations validate the effectiveness of their existing security controls and measures in detecting and preventing cyber attacks. By attempting to circumvent security controls such as firewalls, intrusion detection systems (IDS), and antivirus software, penetration testers can evaluate their resilience and effectiveness in mitigating potential threats. This allows organizations to identify gaps and weaknesses in their security defenses and take proactive measures to strengthen them, such as implementing additional security controls or fine-tuning existing ones.

In addition to identifying vulnerabilities and assessing security controls, penetration testing also helps organizations meet regulatory compliance requirements and industry standards. Many regulatory frameworks, such as the Payment Card Industry Data Security Standard (PCI DSS) and the Health Insurance Portability and Accountability Act (HIPAA), require organizations to conduct regular penetration testing as part of their compliance obligations. By performing penetration testing, organizations can demonstrate compliance with regulatory requirements and ensure the security and integrity of sensitive data.

Moreover, penetration testing helps organizations build resilience against evolving cyber threats and attack techniques by providing hands-on experience with real-world attack scenarios. Penetration testers often leverage the same tools and techniques used by malicious hackers to identify vulnerabilities and exploit security weaknesses, thereby gaining insights into emerging threats and attack vectors. This enables organizations to stay ahead of cyber threats and proactively defend against them, rather than reacting to incidents after they occur.

Additionally, penetration testing helps organizations assess the effectiveness of their incident response procedures and processes in detecting, containing, and responding to security incidents. By simulating cyber attacks and breaches, penetration testers can evaluate how effectively an organization's incident response team detects and responds to security incidents, as well as the adequacy of their incident response plans and procedures. This allows organizations to identify gaps and weaknesses in their incident response capabilities and make improvements to better prepare for and mitigate security incidents.

Furthermore, penetration testing fosters a culture of security awareness and vigilance within an organization by raising awareness about the importance of cybersecurity and the potential risks posed by security vulnerabilities. By involving employees in penetration testing activities and educating them about common security threats and best practices, organizations can empower their workforce to recognize and report potential security issues, thereby enhancing the overall security posture of the organization.

In summary, penetration testing is a critical component of a comprehensive cybersecurity strategy, providing organizations with valuable insights into their security posture, vulnerabilities, and resilience against cyber threats. By identifying and assessing security vulnerabilities, validating security controls, ensuring regulatory compliance, building resilience against emerging threats, evaluating incident response capabilities, and fostering a culture of security awareness, penetration testing helps organizations proactively mitigate security risks and protect their sensitive data and assets from cyber attacks.

Advanced penetration testing strategies encompass a multifaceted approach to assessing and fortifying an organization's security posture against sophisticated cyber threats. Building upon foundational penetration testing methodologies, advanced strategies delve deeper into complex attack vectors, exploit scenarios, and defense evasion techniques. These strategies are essential for organizations seeking to mitigate high-risk vulnerabilities and bolster their resilience in the face of evolving cyber threats.

One advanced strategy employed in penetration testing is the use of custom-built exploits tailored to target specific vulnerabilities within an organization's IT infrastructure. Instead of relying solely on off-the-shelf exploit frameworks, penetration testers may develop custom exploits to bypass security controls, evade detection mechanisms, and gain unauthorized access to critical systems and data. This requires expertise in reverse engineering, vulnerability research, and exploit development, as well as a thorough understanding of the target environment and its unique security challenges.

Furthermore, advanced penetration testing strategies often involve the simulation of advanced persistent threats (APTs) – sophisticated, stealthy adversaries with the capability to infiltrate and compromise high-value targets over extended periods. Penetration testers may emulate APT tactics, techniques, and procedures (TTPs) to assess an organization's resilience against targeted attacks, lateral movement, and data exfiltration. This may include conducting reconnaissance, social engineering, privilege escalation, and persistence techniques to mimic the behavior of real-world adversaries.

Another key aspect of advanced penetration testing strategies is the use of post-exploitation techniques to establish persistent access and maintain control over compromised systems. Once initial access is achieved, penetration testers may employ advanced post-exploitation frameworks such as Metasploit, Empire, or Cobalt Strike to maintain stealth, escalate privileges, and pivot across the network. This allows testers to simulate the actions of skilled adversaries who seek to maintain access and exfiltrate sensitive data without detection.

Moreover, advanced penetration testing strategies often incorporate evasion tactics to bypass security controls such as intrusion detection/prevention systems (IDS/IPS), antivirus software, and endpoint detection and response (EDR) solutions. This may involve obfuscating payloads, encrypting communication channels, and employing polymorphic malware to evade signature-based detection mechanisms. Additionally, penetration testers may leverage living-off-the-land techniques (LOLbins) to execute malicious commands using legitimate system tools and processes, further complicating detection and attribution.

In addition to technical tactics, advanced penetration testing strategies encompass sophisticated social engineering techniques to exploit human vulnerabilities and gain unauthorized access to sensitive information. This may include pretexting, phishing, spear phishing, and impersonation attacks targeting employees, contractors, and other individuals with access to privileged systems and data. By exploiting human psychology and trust relationships, penetration testers can bypass technical controls and infiltrate secure environments.

Furthermore, advanced penetration testing strategies often involve the assessment of cloud-based environments, including infrastructure as a service (IaaS), platform as a service (PaaS), and software as a service (SaaS) offerings. This requires specialized knowledge of cloud architecture, shared responsibility models, and cloud security best practices. Penetration testers may use tools such as AWS Command Line Interface (CLI), Azure PowerShell, or Google Cloud SDK to interact with cloud resources and simulate attacks against cloud-based assets. Additionally, advanced penetration testing strategies encompass the assessment of emerging technologies and attack surfaces, including Internet of Things (IoT) devices, industrial control systems (ICS), and blockchain-based applications. Penetration testers may leverage specialized tools and frameworks tailored to these environments to identify vulnerabilities, assess security controls, and evaluate resilience against targeted attacks.

Furthermore, advanced penetration testing strategies often involve collaboration with red teaming and threat intelligence teams to simulate complex attack scenarios and assess an organization's ability to detect, respond to, and recover from sophisticated cyber threats. This may include conducting purple team exercises, tabletop simulations, and scenario-based training to enhance cross-functional collaboration and incident response readiness.

In summary, advanced penetration testing strategies are essential for organizations seeking to identify and mitigate high-risk security vulnerabilities, assess resilience against sophisticated cyber threats, and enhance overall security posture. By employing custom-built exploits, emulating advanced persistent threats, leveraging post-exploitation techniques, evading detection mechanisms, conducting social engineering attacks, assessing cloud-based environments, and collaborating with red teaming and threat intelligence teams, organizations can proactively identify and address security weaknesses before they can be exploited by adversaries.

Chapter 4: Vulnerability Scanning and Analysis

Vulnerability scanning techniques play a critical role in proactive cybersecurity measures by identifying potential weaknesses and security flaws within an organization's IT infrastructure, applications, and network devices. These techniques involve the use of specialized tools and methodologies to systematically scan, assess, and prioritize vulnerabilities based on their severity and potential impact on the organization's security posture.

One of the primary vulnerability scanning techniques is network scanning, which involves scanning the network infrastructure to identify open ports, services, and potential entry points for attackers. This technique helps organizations gain visibility into their network architecture and identify potential security gaps that could be exploited by malicious actors. Popular tools for network scanning include Nmap, Masscan, and Nessus, which allow security professionals to conduct comprehensive scans and analyze the results to prioritize remediation efforts.

Another important vulnerability scanning technique is web application scanning, which focuses on identifying security vulnerabilities within web applications, such as SQL injection, cross-site scripting (XSS), and insecure authentication mechanisms. Web application scanners such as OWASP ZAP, Burp Suite, and Acunetix are commonly used to crawl web applications, identify vulnerabilities, and provide detailed reports to help developers and security teams address security issues before they can be exploited by attackers.

Furthermore, vulnerability scanning techniques encompass host scanning, which involves scanning individual hosts or endpoints within an organization's network to identify vulnerabilities and misconfigurations. This technique helps organizations identify security weaknesses on specific devices, such as servers, workstations, and IoT devices, and prioritize remediation efforts based on the criticality of the vulnerabilities. Tools such as OpenVAS, Qualys, and Rapid7 InsightVM are commonly used for host scanning and vulnerability assessment.

Additionally, vulnerability scanning techniques include authenticated scanning, which involves scanning systems and applications using valid credentials to access privileged information and perform deeper analysis. Authenticated scanning provides more accurate and comprehensive results by allowing the scanner to access restricted areas of the system and identify vulnerabilities that may not be visible during unauthenticated scans. Tools such as Nessus, Qualys, and Rapid7 InsightVM support authenticated scanning and provide detailed insights into the security posture of systems and applications.

Moreover, vulnerability scanning techniques encompass container scanning, which focuses on identifying vulnerabilities within containerized environments such as Docker, Kubernetes, and OpenShift. Container scanning tools such as Clair, Anchore, and Twistlock are specifically designed to scan container images and identify security vulnerabilities, misconfigurations, and compliance violations. These tools help organizations ensure the security of their containerized applications and mitigate risks associated with container deployments.

Furthermore, vulnerability scanning techniques include cloud infrastructure scanning, which involves scanning cloud-based environments such as AWS, Azure, and Google Cloud Platform (GCP) to identify security vulnerabilities, misconfigurations, and compliance violations. Cloud security posture management (CSPM) tools such as Prisma Cloud, CloudGuard, and CloudCheckr are commonly used to scan cloud infrastructure and provide visibility into security risks across cloud environments.

Additionally, vulnerability scanning techniques encompass continuous monitoring and scanning, which involves regularly scanning IT infrastructure, applications, and network devices to identify new vulnerabilities and security issues as they emerge. Continuous monitoring tools such as Tenable.io, Qualys Continuous Monitoring, and Rapid7 InsightVM enable organizations to proactively detect and remediate vulnerabilities, reducing the window of exposure to potential cyber threats.

Moreover, vulnerability scanning techniques include passive scanning, which involves monitoring network traffic passively to identify vulnerabilities and security issues without actively sending packets or probes to target systems. Passive scanning tools such as Snort, Suricata, and Zeek (formerly known as Bro) analyze network traffic in real-time and detect potential threats based on predefined signatures and behavioral patterns. Passive scanning helps organizations identify and respond to security threats more effectively by providing continuous visibility into network activity.

Furthermore, vulnerability scanning techniques encompass integration with threat intelligence feeds, which involves correlating vulnerability scan results with external threat intelligence sources to prioritize remediation efforts based on the likelihood of exploitation. By integrating vulnerability scanning tools with threat intelligence platforms such as IBM X-Force Exchange, Recorded Future, and Anomali, organizations can better understand the threat landscape and focus their resources on addressing the most critical security risks.

In summary, vulnerability scanning techniques are essential for organizations seeking to identify and mitigate security vulnerabilities within their IT infrastructure, applications, and network devices. By leveraging network scanning, web application scanning, host scanning, authenticated scanning, container scanning, cloud infrastructure scanning, continuous monitoring and scanning, passive scanning, and integration with threat intelligence feeds, organizations can enhance their security posture and reduce the risk of cyber attacks.

Vulnerability analysis methods are crucial components of cybersecurity strategies, enabling organizations to identify, assess, and mitigate security vulnerabilities within their IT infrastructure, applications, and network systems. These methods encompass a variety of techniques and tools designed to systematically analyze vulnerabilities and prioritize remediation efforts based on their severity and potential impact on the organization's security posture.

One fundamental vulnerability analysis method is vulnerability scanning, which involves using automated tools to scan networks, systems, and applications for known vulnerabilities and weaknesses. Tools such as Nessus, OpenVAS, and Qualys Vulnerability Management are widely used for vulnerability scanning, allowing security teams to conduct comprehensive scans and generate reports detailing identified vulnerabilities.

Another important vulnerability analysis method is penetration testing, also known as ethical hacking, which involves simulating real-world cyber attacks to identify vulnerabilities and assess the effectiveness of security controls. Penetration testing tools such as Metasploit, Burp Suite, and Nmap are commonly used by security professionals to identify weaknesses in networks, applications, and infrastructure and provide recommendations for remediation.

Furthermore, vulnerability analysis methods include manual code review, which involves manually inspecting source code for security vulnerabilities and coding errors that may introduce security risks. Manual code review requires expertise in programming languages and security best practices and is often performed by skilled software developers or security professionals using integrated development environment (IDE) tools such as Visual Studio Code, IntelliJ IDEA, and Eclipse.

Additionally, vulnerability analysis methods encompass static code analysis, which involves analyzing source code without executing the program to identify potential security vulnerabilities, coding errors, and compliance violations. Static code analysis tools such as SonarQube, Checkmarx, and Fortify are commonly used to scan source code for common security issues such as SQL injection, cross-site scripting (XSS), and buffer overflows.

Moreover, vulnerability analysis methods include dynamic code analysis, which involves analyzing the behavior of a program during runtime to identify security vulnerabilities, memory leaks, and other runtime errors. Dynamic code analysis tools such as Valgrind, AFL (American Fuzzy Lop), and WinDbg are commonly used to perform runtime analysis and identify security vulnerabilities in software applications.

Furthermore, vulnerability analysis methods encompass fuzz testing, also known as fuzzing, which involves sending malformed or unexpected inputs to software applications to identify vulnerabilities and trigger unexpected behavior. Fuzz testing tools such as AFL (American Fuzzy Lop), Peach Fuzzer, and Radamsa are commonly used to automate the process of generating and sending fuzzed inputs to target applications and analyzing the results for potential vulnerabilities.

Additionally, vulnerability analysis methods include threat modeling, which involves systematically identifying and prioritizing potential threats to an organization's assets, applications, and infrastructure and designing security controls to mitigate these threats. Threat modeling techniques such as STRIDE (Spoofing, Tampering, Repudiation, Information disclosure, Denial of Service, Elevation of privilege) and DREAD (Damage, Reproducibility, Exploitability, Affected users, Discoverability) are commonly used to assess the security risks associated with software applications and prioritize remediation efforts.

Moreover, vulnerability analysis methods encompass security architecture review, which involves reviewing the design and implementation of an organization's security architecture to identify potential vulnerabilities and weaknesses. Security architecture review requires expertise in cybersecurity best practices and is often performed by experienced security architects or consultants using documentation, diagrams, and interviews with key stakeholders.

Furthermore, vulnerability analysis methods include compliance auditing, which involves assessing an organization's compliance with regulatory requirements, industry standards, and security best practices to identify potential vulnerabilities and gaps in security controls. Compliance auditing tools such as Nessus Compliance Checks, OpenSCAP, and Lynis are commonly used to automate the process of assessing compliance with standards such as PCI DSS, HIPAA, and ISO 27001.

In summary, vulnerability analysis methods are essential for organizations seeking to identify and mitigate security vulnerabilities within their IT infrastructure, applications, and network systems. By leveraging vulnerability scanning, penetration testing, manual code review, static code analysis, dynamic code analysis, fuzz testing, threat modeling, security architecture review, and compliance auditing, organizations can enhance their security posture and reduce the risk of cyber attacks.

Chapter 5: Threat Intelligence Integration

Incorporating threat intelligence into cybersecurity strategies is crucial for organizations aiming to enhance their security posture and effectively defend against cyber threats. Threat intelligence refers to actionable information about potential or current cyber threats that can help organizations understand the tactics, techniques, and procedures (TTPs) employed by threat actors, as well as the vulnerabilities they target. By integrating threat intelligence into their security operations, organizations can proactively identify and mitigate security risks, detect and respond to cyber threats more effectively, and make informed decisions to protect their assets, data, and reputation.

One common approach to incorporating threat intelligence is through the use of threat intelligence feeds, which provide organizations with real-time or near-real-time information about known threats, indicators of compromise (IOCs), and malicious activities observed across the global threat landscape. These feeds can be obtained from commercial threat intelligence providers, open-source intelligence (OSINT) platforms, government agencies, industry groups, and information sharing and analysis centers (ISACs). Organizations can subscribe to threat intelligence feeds relevant to their industry, geography, and specific threat landscape to receive timely updates about emerging threats and vulnerabilities.

To integrate threat intelligence feeds into their security operations, organizations can use security information and event management (SIEM) systems, threat intelligence platforms (TIPs), or security orchestration, automation, and response (SOAR) solutions. These platforms allow organizations to ingest, normalize, and correlate threat intelligence feeds with their existing security data sources, such as logs, alerts, and network traffic, to identify potential threats and prioritize response actions. By automatically correlating threat intelligence with security events, organizations can improve their ability to detect and respond to cyber threats in real time.

Another approach to incorporating threat intelligence is through the use of threat intelligence sharing and collaboration platforms, which facilitate the exchange of threat information among trusted partners, peers, and industry stakeholders. These platforms enable organizations to share threat intelligence, indicators of compromise (IOCs), malware samples, and best practices for threat detection and mitigation. By participating in threat intelligence sharing communities, organizations can gain access to a broader range of threat intelligence sources, enhance their situational awareness, and collaborate with other organizations to collectively defend against cyber threats.

Furthermore, organizations can leverage threat intelligence to enhance their incident response capabilities and improve their ability to respond to cyber incidents effectively. By enriching security alerts and incident data with contextual information from threat intelligence feeds, organizations can better understand the nature and severity of security incidents, prioritize response efforts, and take timely action to contain and remediate threats. Additionally, threat intelligence can provide valuable insights into the tactics, techniques, and procedures (TTPs) used by threat actors, enabling organizations to develop more effective incident response playbooks and countermeasures.

Moreover, threat intelligence can play a crucial role in informing risk management and decision-making processes within organizations. By analyzing threat intelligence data alongside information about their own assets, vulnerabilities, and security controls, organizations can identify gaps in their defenses, assess their exposure to specific threats, and allocate resources more effectively to mitigate risks. Threat intelligence can also provide valuable insights into emerging trends and evolving cyber threats, helping organizations anticipate and prepare for future security challenges.

In summary, incorporating threat intelligence into cybersecurity strategies is essential for organizations seeking to enhance their security posture, detect and respond to cyber threats effectively, and make informed decisions to protect their assets and data. By leveraging threat intelligence feeds, sharing and collaboration platforms, incident response capabilities, and risk management processes, organizations can gain valuable insights into the threat landscape, improve their ability to detect and mitigate security risks, and strengthen their overall cyber resilience.

Threat intelligence analysis techniques are critical for organizations looking to extract actionable insights from the vast amount of threat data available and effectively defend against cyber threats. These techniques encompass a range of methodologies and tools aimed at collecting, processing, analyzing, and interpreting threat intelligence to identify potential risks, understand threat actors' motives and tactics, and make informed decisions to mitigate security threats.

One fundamental aspect of threat intelligence analysis is data collection, which involves gathering information from various sources, including open-source intelligence (OSINT), commercial threat feeds, government agencies, industry groups, and information sharing and analysis centers (ISACs). Organizations can use a variety of tools and techniques to collect threat intelligence data, such as web scraping, data mining, and automated data collection scripts. Additionally, organizations can leverage threat intelligence platforms (TIPs) to aggregate and normalize threat data from multiple sources, making it easier to analyze and correlate.

Once threat data is collected, the next step in threat intelligence analysis is data processing and enrichment. This involves cleaning and normalizing the data to ensure consistency and accuracy, as well as enriching the data with additional context, such as threat actor profiles, attack techniques, and indicators of compromise (IOCs). Tools like MISP (Malware Information Sharing Platform) and TAXII (Trusted Automated Exchange of Indicator Information) can be used to standardize and share threat intelligence data, while tools like STIX (Structured Threat Information eXpression) and CybOX (Cyber Observable eXpression) provide a standardized format for representing threat information.

Once the threat data is processed and enriched, the next step is data analysis, which involves examining the data to identify patterns, trends, and anomalies that may indicate potential security threats. This can involve various analytical techniques, such as statistical analysis, data visualization, and machine learning algorithms. Organizations can use tools like Elasticsearch, Kibana, and Splunk for log analysis and data visualization, while machine learning algorithms can be used to identify unusual patterns or behaviors indicative of malicious activity.

One common approach to threat intelligence analysis is indicator-based analysis, which focuses on identifying specific indicators of compromise (IOCs) associated with known threats, such as IP addresses, domain names, file hashes, and malware signatures. Organizations can use tools like YARA (Yet Another Recursive Acronym) for malware detection and IOC identification, as well as threat intelligence feeds and databases like VirusTotal and OpenIOC (Open Indicators of Compromise) to search for known IOCs.

Another approach to threat intelligence analysis is adversary-based analysis, which focuses on understanding the tactics, techniques, and procedures (TTPs) employed by threat actors to carry out cyber attacks. This involves profiling threat actors and analyzing their motives, capabilities, and attack patterns to anticipate and defend against future attacks. Tools like MITRE ATT&CK (Adversarial Tactics, Techniques, and Common Knowledge) provide a framework for mapping adversary TTPs and identifying gaps in defenses.

Additionally, behavioral analysis techniques can be used to identify anomalous or suspicious behavior indicative of a security threat. This involves monitoring and analyzing user and network activity to detect deviations from normal behavior, such as unauthorized access attempts, unusual file transfers, and network anomalies. Tools like Security Information and Event Management (SIEM) systems and User and Entity Behavior Analytics (UEBA) platforms can be used for behavioral analysis and anomaly detection.

Furthermore, threat intelligence analysis can benefit from collaborative analysis techniques, which involve sharing threat intelligence data and insights with trusted partners, peers, and industry stakeholders. By collaborating with other organizations, sharing information about emerging threats and attack trends, and leveraging collective expertise and resources, organizations can enhance their situational awareness and improve their ability to detect and respond to cyber threats effectively.

In summary, threat intelligence analysis techniques play a crucial role in helping organizations identify and mitigate security threats effectively. By collecting, processing, analyzing, and interpreting threat intelligence data using a variety of tools and techniques, organizations can gain valuable insights into the threat landscape, understand adversary tactics and techniques, and make informed decisions to protect their assets and data from cyber threats.

Chapter 6: Secure Development Lifecycle Integration

The Secure Development Lifecycle (SDL) is a systematic approach to integrating security practices into the software development process from the initial planning phases through deployment and maintenance. It is designed to identify and mitigate security risks early in the development lifecycle, reducing the likelihood of security vulnerabilities and breaches in the final product.

One of the foundational principles of the SDL is that security should be considered at every stage of the development process, starting with the requirements gathering phase. During this phase, security requirements are identified based on the anticipated threats and risks to the software application. This may include specifying authentication mechanisms, access controls, data encryption requirements, and other security features necessary to protect the application and its users.

Once security requirements are defined, they are incorporated into the design phase of the SDL. Developers work to design the architecture and components of the software application with security in mind, considering factors such as input validation, error handling, and secure communication protocols. Threat modeling techniques, such as creating attack trees or data flow diagrams, may be used to identify potential security vulnerabilities and design appropriate countermeasures to mitigate them.

As development progresses, secure coding practices are applied to implement the design in a secure manner. This includes following coding standards and best practices for writing secure code, such as input validation, output encoding, parameterized queries to prevent SQL injection, and using secure libraries and frameworks. Static code analysis tools, such as FindBugs, SonarQube, or ESLint, can be used to automatically identify security vulnerabilities in the codebase and provide developers with actionable feedback to remediate them.

In addition to secure coding practices, developers must also conduct security testing throughout the development process to identify and address security issues early on. This includes both manual and automated security testing techniques, such as penetration testing, security code reviews, and dynamic application security testing (DAST). Tools like Burp Suite, OWASP ZAP, and Nessus can be used to automate security testing and identify common security vulnerabilities, such as cross-site scripting (XSS), SQL injection, and insecure authentication mechanisms.

Once the software application is developed, it undergoes a thorough security review to ensure that all security requirements have been met and that no critical security vulnerabilities remain. This may involve conducting a final round of security testing, as well as reviewing the codebase and architecture for compliance with security standards and best practices. Security audits and code reviews are often conducted by independent third-party security experts to provide an unbiased assessment of the software's security posture.

After the software application is deployed, ongoing security monitoring and maintenance are essential to detect and respond to new security threats and vulnerabilities that may arise over time. This includes monitoring for security incidents, applying security patches and updates to the software and its dependencies, and regularly reviewing and updating security policies and procedures. Security information and event management (SIEM) systems, intrusion detection systems (IDS), and antivirus software can be used to monitor for suspicious activity and respond to security incidents in real-time.

In summary, the Secure Development Lifecycle (SDL) is a systematic approach to integrating security practices into the software development process from start to finish. By incorporating security considerations into every phase of the development lifecycle and employing a combination of secure coding practices, security testing techniques, and ongoing security monitoring and maintenance, organizations can develop software applications that are more resilient to security threats and better protect the confidentiality, integrity, and availability of their data and systems.

Integrating security into the development lifecycle is essential for building robust and secure software applications that can withstand the ever-evolving landscape of cyber threats. This integration ensures that security considerations are addressed at every stage of the software development process, from initial design to deployment and maintenance.

The first step in integrating security into the development lifecycle is to establish a set of security requirements and guidelines that developers must follow throughout the development process. These requirements may include specific security features that need to be implemented, compliance with industry standards and regulations, and best practices for secure coding.

One way to enforce security requirements is to incorporate them into the project management and development tools used by the development team. For example, security requirements can be added to the project backlog or user stories in Agile project management tools like Jira or Trello. This ensures that security considerations are prioritized alongside other development tasks and are not overlooked during the development process.

As development progresses, security considerations are integrated into the design phase of the development lifecycle. This involves identifying potential security risks and vulnerabilities in the software architecture and designing appropriate countermeasures to mitigate them. Threat modeling techniques, such as creating attack trees or data flow diagrams, can be used to identify potential security threats and prioritize security controls based on their potential impact.

During the implementation phase, developers follow secure coding practices to ensure that security vulnerabilities are not inadvertently introduced into the codebase. This includes practices such as input validation, output encoding, and secure error handling to prevent common vulnerabilities such as cross-site scripting (XSS), SQL injection, and buffer overflows. Static code analysis tools like Checkmarx or Fortify can be used to automatically identify security vulnerabilities in the code and provide developers with feedback on how to remediate them.

In addition to secure coding practices, developers also conduct security testing throughout the development process to identify and address security issues early on. This includes both manual and automated security testing techniques, such as penetration testing, security code reviews, and dynamic application security testing (DAST). Tools like Burp Suite, OWASP ZAP, and Nessus can be used to automate security testing and identify common security vulnerabilities in the application.

Once the software is developed, it undergoes a thorough security review to ensure that all security requirements have been met and that no critical security vulnerabilities remain. This may involve conducting a final round of security testing, as well as reviewing the codebase and architecture for compliance with security standards and best practices. Security audits and code reviews are often conducted by independent third-party security experts to provide an unbiased assessment of the software's security posture.

After the software is deployed, ongoing security monitoring and maintenance are essential to detect and respond to new security threats and vulnerabilities that may arise over time. This includes monitoring for security incidents, applying security patches and updates to the software and its dependencies, and regularly reviewing and updating security policies and procedures.

In summary, integrating security into the development lifecycle is essential for building secure software applications that can withstand the ever-evolving landscape of cyber threats. By incorporating security considerations into every phase of the development process and employing a combination of secure coding practices, security testing techniques, and ongoing security monitoring and maintenance, organizations can develop software applications that are more resilient to security threats and better protect the confidentiality, integrity, and availability of their data and systems.

Chapter 7: Advanced Test Environment Configuration

Advanced test environment setup is crucial for ensuring the reliability and accuracy of software testing processes, especially in complex and dynamic software development environments. It involves creating a controlled and representative environment that closely mimics the production environment, allowing for thorough testing of software applications in a realistic setting.

One key aspect of advanced test environment setup is infrastructure as code (IaC), which enables the automated provisioning and configuration of test environments using code. Tools like Terraform and AWS CloudFormation allow developers to define the infrastructure requirements of the test environment in code, specifying the resources, networking configurations, and dependencies needed for testing. By codifying the infrastructure setup, teams can easily replicate and deploy consistent test environments across different stages of the development lifecycle.

Containerization technologies such as Docker and Kubernetes are also integral to advanced test environment setup, enabling the creation of lightweight and isolated environments for testing. Docker allows developers to package applications and their dependencies into portable containers, which can be easily deployed and managed across different environments. Kubernetes provides orchestration capabilities for managing containerized applications at scale, allowing teams to automate the deployment, scaling, and monitoring of test environments.

In addition to infrastructure automation and containerization, version control systems like Git play a crucial role in advanced test environment setup. By storing infrastructure code and configuration files in version control repositories, teams can track changes, collaborate effectively, and maintain a history of modifications to the test environment setup. This ensures consistency and repeatability across different test environments and allows for easy rollback to previous configurations if needed.

Another important aspect of advanced test environment setup is the use of configuration management tools such as Ansible, Chef, and Puppet. These tools automate the configuration and management of software components and system settings within the test environment, ensuring consistency and reliability across different instances. Configuration management scripts can be used to automate the installation of software packages, the configuration of network settings, and the setup of user accounts, among other tasks.

Infrastructure monitoring and logging are essential components of advanced test environment setup, providing visibility into the health and performance of the test environment during testing. Tools like Prometheus, Grafana, and ELK stack (Elasticsearch, Logstash, Kibana) allow teams to monitor key metrics, analyze logs, and troubleshoot issues in real-time. By proactively monitoring the test environment, teams can identify performance bottlenecks, resource constraints, and other issues that may impact testing outcomes.

Security is another critical consideration in advanced test environment setup, especially when testing sensitive or regulated applications. Teams must ensure that test environments are securely configured and isolated from production systems to prevent unauthorized access and data breaches. Techniques such as network segmentation, encryption, and access controls help mitigate security risks and protect sensitive data during testing.

Finally, continuous integration and continuous deployment (CI/CD) pipelines play a vital role in advanced test environment setup, enabling automated testing and deployment of software changes. CI/CD pipelines automate the build, test, and deployment processes, allowing teams to rapidly iterate on code changes and deliver updates to the test environment quickly and reliably. Tools like Jenkins, GitLab CI/CD, and CircleCI are commonly used to orchestrate CI/CD pipelines and streamline the software delivery process.

In summary, advanced test environment setup is essential for ensuring the reliability, repeatability, and security of software testing processes. By leveraging infrastructure automation, containerization, configuration management, monitoring, and security best practices, teams can create robust and scalable test environments that support agile development practices and accelerate the delivery of high-quality software applications.

Test environment optimization strategies are crucial for enhancing the efficiency, reliability, and scalability of software testing processes. These strategies encompass various techniques and best practices aimed at streamlining the setup, configuration, and management of test environments to maximize resource utilization and minimize bottlenecks.

One key aspect of test environment optimization is infrastructure automation using tools like Terraform, Ansible, and Puppet. These tools enable the automated provisioning and configuration of test environments, allowing teams to quickly spin up and tear down environments as needed. By defining infrastructure requirements in code, teams can ensure consistency across environments and eliminate manual configuration errors.

Containerization technologies such as Docker and Kubernetes are also instrumental in test environment optimization. Containers provide lightweight, isolated environments for running tests, making it easier to replicate and scale test environments as workload demands change. Docker Compose allows developers to define multi-container applications in a single configuration file, simplifying the setup of complex test environments with multiple interconnected services.

Virtualization platforms like VMware and VirtualBox offer another avenue for test environment optimization. By virtualizing hardware resources, teams can create isolated environments for testing different configurations and scenarios without the need for physical hardware. Virtual machines (VMs) can be easily cloned and snapshot, allowing teams to create and restore test environments quickly.

Cloud computing platforms such as AWS, Azure, and Google Cloud provide scalable and on-demand infrastructure for test environment optimization. With cloud services, teams can provision virtual machines, storage, and networking resources in minutes, reducing the time and effort required to set up test environments.

Infrastructure as code (IaC) tools like AWS CloudFormation and Azure Resource Manager further automate the deployment and management of cloud-based test environments.

Continuous integration (CI) and continuous deployment (CD) pipelines are essential components of test environment optimization. By automating the build, test, and deployment processes, CI/CD pipelines enable teams to rapidly iterate on code changes and deliver updates to test environments. Jenkins, GitLab CI/CD, and CircleCI are popular CI/CD tools that orchestrate the automation of testing and deployment tasks.

Performance testing and optimization are critical aspects of test environment optimization, particularly for applications that require high throughput and low latency. Tools like Apache JMeter and Gatling are used to simulate load and stress conditions on applications, helping identify performance bottlenecks and scalability issues. By optimizing code, database queries, and network configurations, teams can ensure that applications perform optimally under various conditions.

Monitoring and analytics tools play a crucial role in test environment optimization by providing visibility into the health and performance of test environments. Tools like Prometheus, Grafana, and ELK stack allow teams to monitor key metrics, analyze logs, and detect anomalies in real-time. By proactively monitoring test environments, teams can identify and address issues before they impact testing outcomes.

Security is another important consideration in test environment optimization. Teams must ensure that test environments are securely configured and isolated from production systems to prevent unauthorized access and data breaches. Techniques such as network segmentation, encryption, and access controls help mitigate security risks and protect sensitive data during testing.

In summary, test environment optimization is essential for maximizing the efficiency, reliability, and scalability of software testing processes. By leveraging infrastructure automation, containerization, virtualization, cloud computing, CI/CD pipelines, performance testing, monitoring, and security best practices, teams can create robust and scalable test environments that support agile development practices and accelerate the delivery of high-quality software applications.

Chapter 8: Compliance Testing Strategies

Compliance testing is a critical aspect of software development and deployment, ensuring that applications adhere to regulatory requirements, industry standards, and organizational policies. It involves verifying that software systems meet specific criteria related to security, privacy, accessibility, and other legal or regulatory obligations. Compliance testing encompasses a range of activities aimed at assessing the conformity of software products with relevant standards and regulations.

One of the primary purposes of compliance testing is to mitigate risks associated with non-compliance, such as legal penalties, financial losses, reputational damage, and security breaches. By conducting thorough compliance testing, organizations can demonstrate their commitment to maintaining integrity, confidentiality, and availability of data, thereby building trust with customers, partners, and regulatory authorities.

The first step in compliance testing is to identify applicable regulations, standards, and contractual requirements that govern the software under test. This may include industry-specific regulations like HIPAA for healthcare or GDPR for data privacy, as well as general standards such as ISO 27001 for information security management. Organizations must stay abreast of changes in regulatory landscape to ensure ongoing compliance with evolving requirements.

Once the regulatory landscape is understood, organizations can define compliance requirements and develop test plans to verify adherence to those requirements. Test cases are designed to cover various aspects of compliance, including data security, authentication mechanisms, encryption protocols, access controls, audit trails, and data retention policies. Automated testing tools such as OWASP ZAP, Nessus, and Burp Suite can be used to scan applications for security vulnerabilities and compliance gaps.

In addition to technical testing, compliance testing may also involve documentation reviews, interviews with stakeholders, and on-site audits to validate compliance with regulatory requirements. Documentation reviews assess the adequacy and completeness of policies, procedures, and controls implemented to meet compliance obligations. Interviews with stakeholders provide insights into organizational practices and processes related to compliance.

Continuous monitoring and periodic assessments are essential components of compliance testing to ensure ongoing compliance with regulatory requirements. Organizations should regularly review and update their compliance testing procedures in response to changes in regulations, technology, and business practices. This iterative approach helps organizations identify and address compliance gaps in a timely manner.

Compliance testing is particularly important in industries where regulations are stringent and non-compliance can have severe consequences. For example, in the financial services sector, organizations must comply with regulations such as PCI DSS for payment card security, Sarbanes-Oxley Act (SOX) for financial reporting, and Basel III for banking regulations. Failure to comply with these regulations can result in significant fines, legal sanctions, and damage to reputation.

In the healthcare industry, compliance with regulations such as HIPAA is critical to protecting patient privacy and ensuring the security of electronic health records (EHRs). Healthcare organizations must implement appropriate safeguards to protect sensitive patient information from unauthorized access, disclosure, and tampering. Compliance testing helps healthcare organizations identify vulnerabilities in their systems and processes and implement remediation measures to address them.

Similarly, in the e-commerce sector, organizations must comply with regulations such as the EU General Data Protection Regulation (GDPR) to protect consumer privacy and data rights. Compliance testing ensures that organizations collect, process, and store customer data in accordance with GDPR requirements, thereby minimizing the risk of data breaches and regulatory penalties.

In summary, compliance testing is essential for ensuring that software systems comply with regulatory requirements, industry standards, and organizational policies. By conducting thorough compliance testing, organizations can identify and mitigate risks associated with non-compliance, protect sensitive data, and build trust with customers, partners, and regulatory authorities. Compliance testing is an ongoing process that requires continuous monitoring, periodic assessments, and proactive measures to address evolving regulatory requirements and emerging threats.

Compliance testing is an indispensable aspect of software development and deployment, ensuring that applications meet specific regulatory requirements, industry standards, and organizational policies. To conduct effective compliance testing, organizations need to employ comprehensive strategies that cover various aspects of regulatory compliance and address potential risks and challenges. These strategies encompass several key elements, including thorough planning, clear documentation, robust testing methodologies, automation, and continuous improvement.

A crucial aspect of effective compliance testing is meticulous planning and preparation. Organizations should begin by identifying relevant regulations, standards, and contractual obligations that apply to their software products. This involves conducting a comprehensive analysis of legal and regulatory requirements at the local, national, and international levels. Once the regulatory landscape is understood, organizations can define compliance objectives, establish test criteria, and develop test plans and procedures tailored to meet specific compliance goals.

Clear documentation is essential for effective compliance testing. Organizations should maintain detailed records of compliance requirements, test cases, test results, and remediation activities. Documentation serves as evidence of compliance efforts and provides a basis for audit trails, regulatory reporting, and stakeholder communication. Tools such as Jira, Confluence, and SharePoint can be used to manage and document compliance testing activities, ensuring transparency, traceability, and accountability throughout the testing process.

Robust testing methodologies are critical for ensuring the accuracy, reliability, and effectiveness of compliance testing efforts. Organizations should employ a combination of manual and automated testing techniques to verify compliance with regulatory requirements. Manual testing involves human intervention to validate specific aspects of compliance, such as data security, privacy controls, and access permissions. Automated testing tools such as Selenium, Appium, and SoapUI can be used to automate repetitive testing tasks, accelerate testing cycles, and improve test coverage.

In addition to functional testing, organizations should also perform non-functional testing to assess the performance, reliability, and scalability of software systems under compliance constraints. This includes testing for security vulnerabilities, resilience to cyber attacks, and adherence to industry best practices for secure coding and configuration management. Tools such as Nessus, Qualys, and OpenVAS can be used to conduct vulnerability assessments and penetration testing to identify and remediate security weaknesses.

Automation is key to scaling compliance testing efforts and ensuring consistency and repeatability across different environments and configurations. By automating routine testing tasks, organizations can minimize manual errors, reduce testing time, and increase test coverage. Continuous integration (CI) and continuous deployment (CD) pipelines can be integrated with automated testing frameworks to enable continuous testing and validation of software changes as they are deployed to production environments.

Continuous improvement is essential for optimizing compliance testing processes and staying ahead of evolving regulatory requirements and industry trends. Organizations should regularly review and evaluate their compliance testing practices, identify areas for improvement, and implement corrective actions to address deficiencies. This iterative approach enables organizations to adapt to changing compliance requirements, mitigate emerging risks, and enhance the effectiveness of their compliance testing programs.

Furthermore, organizations should foster a culture of compliance and accountability throughout the organization by providing training and awareness programs for employees, contractors, and other stakeholders. By promoting a shared understanding of compliance objectives and responsibilities, organizations can cultivate a proactive approach to compliance testing and empower individuals to contribute to compliance efforts effectively.

In summary, effective compliance testing requires comprehensive strategies that encompass thorough planning, clear documentation, robust testing methodologies, automation, and continuous improvement. By adopting these strategies, organizations can ensure that their software products comply with regulatory requirements, industry standards, and organizational policies, thereby minimizing legal and financial risks, protecting sensitive data, and building trust with customers, partners, and regulatory authorities. Compliance testing is an ongoing process that requires diligence, collaboration, and commitment to excellence.

Chapter 9: Incident Response Simulation

Simulating incident response scenarios is a critical aspect of proactive cybersecurity preparedness for organizations across various industries. These simulations, also known as tabletop exercises or incident response drills, involve creating realistic scenarios to test an organization's ability to detect, respond to, and recover from cybersecurity incidents effectively. By simulating different types of cyberattacks, such as data breaches, ransomware infections, and denial-of-service (DoS) attacks, organizations can identify vulnerabilities, validate response plans, and improve incident response capabilities.

The first step in simulating incident response scenarios is to define the objectives and scope of the exercise. This involves identifying the specific scenarios to be simulated, the participants involved, and the desired outcomes. Scenarios should be based on real-world threats and tailored to the organization's industry, business processes, and IT infrastructure. For example, a financial institution may simulate a scenario involving a targeted phishing attack aimed at stealing customer financial data, while a healthcare provider may simulate a scenario involving a ransomware attack targeting patient records.

Once the scenarios are defined, participants are assigned roles and responsibilities based on their roles within the organization's incident response team. This typically includes representatives from IT, security, legal, human resources, communications, and executive management. Each participant is given specific tasks and objectives to complete during the simulation, such as detecting the incident, containing the damage, notifying stakeholders, and initiating recovery efforts.

During the simulation, facilitators orchestrate the scenario by presenting participants with a series of simulated events and challenges designed to mimic the progression of a real cyberattack. These events may include the discovery of suspicious network activity, the identification of compromised systems, the loss of critical data, and the activation of incident response procedures. Facilitators can use various tools and techniques to simulate these events, including threat intelligence feeds, simulated malware, and network traffic generators.

Participants are required to respond to each simulated event in real-time, following established incident response procedures and protocols. This may involve conducting forensic investigations, isolating affected systems, implementing containment measures, and coordinating with external stakeholders, such as law enforcement, regulatory agencies, and third-party vendors. Throughout the simulation, participants must communicate effectively, share information, and collaborate to mitigate the impact of the incident and restore normal operations.

One of the key benefits of simulating incident response scenarios is that it allows organizations to identify weaknesses and gaps in their incident response plans and procedures. By observing how participants respond to simulated events, organizations can identify areas for improvement, such as inadequate detection capabilities, slow response times, ineffective communication channels, and insufficient coordination between internal teams and external partners. These insights can then be used to refine incident response plans, enhance training programs, and allocate resources more effectively.

Furthermore, simulating incident response scenarios helps organizations build confidence in their incident response capabilities and prepare for the unexpected. By practicing responses to different types of cyberattacks in a controlled environment, organizations can build muscle memory, improve decision-making skills, and reduce the likelihood of panic or confusion during a real incident. This proactive approach to cybersecurity preparedness can help organizations minimize the impact of cyberattacks, reduce downtime, and protect sensitive data and critical assets.

In summary, simulating incident response scenarios is a valuable exercise for organizations seeking to enhance their cybersecurity preparedness and resilience. By creating realistic scenarios and engaging participants in simulated cyberattacks, organizations can identify weaknesses in their incident response plans, improve response capabilities, and build confidence in their ability to detect, respond to, and recover from cybersecurity incidents. By investing in regular incident response simulations, organizations can better protect themselves against cyber threats and minimize the potential impact of cyberattacks on their operations and reputation.

Incident response exercise planning is a critical component of any organization's cybersecurity strategy, helping to ensure that teams are prepared to effectively detect, respond to, and recover from cyber incidents. These exercises, also known as tabletop exercises or incident response drills, simulate real-world scenarios to test the organization's incident response capabilities and identify areas for improvement. Effective planning is essential to the success of these exercises, as it helps organizations define objectives, establish roles and responsibilities, and create realistic scenarios tailored to their specific needs.

The first step in incident response exercise planning is to define the objectives and scope of the exercise. This involves identifying the goals that the organization aims to achieve through the exercise, such as validating incident response procedures, testing communication channels, or assessing the effectiveness of existing security controls. Objectives should be specific, measurable, achievable, relevant, and time-bound (SMART), providing clear guidance for the planning and execution of the exercise.

Once the objectives are established, the next step is to assemble a cross-functional team to plan and execute the exercise. This team typically includes representatives from IT, security, legal, human resources, communications, and executive management, reflecting the diverse stakeholders involved in incident response activities. Each team member brings unique expertise and perspectives to the planning process, helping to ensure that the exercise addresses all relevant aspects of incident response.

With the team in place, the next phase of planning involves identifying the scenarios to be simulated during the exercise. Scenarios should be based on realistic threats and tailored to the organization's industry, business processes, and IT environment. Common scenarios include data breaches, ransomware attacks, insider threats, and denial-of-service (DoS) attacks. Scenarios can be developed internally or adapted from publicly available threat intelligence sources, such as the MITRE ATT&CK framework or industry-specific threat reports. Once the scenarios are defined, the planning team works to create a detailed exercise plan outlining the sequence of events, the roles and responsibilities of participants, and the specific tasks to be performed during the exercise. This plan serves as a roadmap for the execution of the exercise, providing guidance for facilitators, participants, and observers. It should include key milestones, timelines, and success criteria to measure the effectiveness of the exercise and evaluate performance against established objectives.

In addition to planning the scenarios and logistics of the exercise, incident response exercise planning also involves selecting the appropriate tools and resources to support the simulation. This may include incident response playbooks, communication templates, incident response platforms, and collaboration tools. These resources help participants navigate the simulated incidents, communicate effectively, and document their actions and decisions throughout the exercise.

As part of the planning process, organizations should also consider the logistics of conducting the exercise, including scheduling, location, and participant availability. Depending on the size and complexity of the organization, exercises may be conducted onsite, remotely, or in a hybrid format, with participants joining from multiple locations. It's essential to ensure that the necessary technology infrastructure and support are in place to facilitate remote participation and collaboration during the exercise.

Once the exercise plan is finalized, the planning team conducts a thorough review and validation to ensure that all aspects of the exercise have been adequately addressed. This may involve conducting walkthroughs or dry runs of the scenarios, soliciting feedback from stakeholders, and making any necessary adjustments or refinements to the plan. Finally, the exercise plan is executed according to the established timeline and objectives. Facilitators guide participants through the simulated scenarios, presenting them with a series of events and challenges to respond to in real-time. Participants are expected to follow established incident response procedures, communicate effectively, and collaborate to mitigate the impact of the simulated incidents. Throughout the exercise, facilitators and observers monitor participant performance, document observations, and collect feedback for post-exercise analysis. After the exercise concludes, the planning team conducts a comprehensive debriefing session to review the exercise outcomes, identify lessons learned, and develop action plans for addressing any gaps or deficiencies identified during the exercise.

In summary, incident response exercise planning is a critical process that helps organizations prepare for cyber incidents by simulating realistic scenarios and testing their incident response capabilities. By defining objectives, assembling a cross-functional team, developing realistic scenarios, and selecting appropriate tools and resources, organizations can conduct effective exercises that enhance their readiness to detect, respond to, and recover from cyber incidents.

Chapter 10: Comprehensive System Testing and Security Frameworks

Comprehensive testing frameworks play a pivotal role in software development by providing a structured approach to ensure the quality, reliability, and functionality of software applications. These frameworks encompass various methodologies, tools, and techniques aimed at systematically validating the behavior and performance of software systems across different stages of the development lifecycle. From unit testing to end-to-end testing, comprehensive testing frameworks help identify defects early, facilitate efficient bug fixing, and ultimately deliver robust and high-quality software products to end-users.

At the heart of comprehensive testing frameworks lie the principles of automation, repeatability, and scalability. Automation enables the execution of tests with minimal human intervention, allowing for faster feedback loops and more frequent testing cycles. By automating repetitive test scenarios, developers and testers can focus on more complex and critical aspects of testing, such as exploratory testing and edge case scenarios. Moreover, automation enhances the reliability and consistency of test execution, reducing the risk of human error and ensuring accurate results across different environments and configurations.

One of the most widely adopted comprehensive testing frameworks is the Test-Driven Development (TDD) approach, which advocates writing automated tests before implementing the corresponding functionality. In TDD, developers start by writing a failing test that defines the desired behavior of a specific feature or component. They then write the minimum amount of code necessary to make the test pass, followed by refactoring to improve the code's design and maintainability. This iterative process ensures that each new feature is thoroughly tested and validated against the expected behavior, leading to cleaner code, fewer defects, and faster development cycles.

Another essential component of comprehensive testing frameworks is Continuous Integration (CI) and Continuous Deployment (CD) pipelines, which automate the build, test, and deployment processes to achieve rapid and reliable software delivery. CI/CD pipelines enable developers to integrate code changes frequently, run automated tests in a controlled environment, and deploy changes to production with confidence. By automating these processes, CI/CD pipelines help identify integration issues early, ensure code quality throughout the development lifecycle, and accelerate time-to-market for software releases.

In addition to unit testing and integration testing, comprehensive testing frameworks encompass a wide range of testing techniques, including functional testing, performance testing, security testing, and usability testing. Functional testing ensures that the software meets the specified requirements and behaves as expected from the end-user's perspective. Performance testing evaluates the system's responsiveness, scalability, and reliability under different load conditions, helping identify performance bottlenecks and optimize resource utilization. Security testing focuses on identifying vulnerabilities and weaknesses in the software that could be exploited by malicious actors, such as SQL injection, cross-site scripting (XSS), and authentication bypass vulnerabilities. Usability testing evaluates the software's user interface and user experience (UI/UX) design to ensure that it is intuitive, accessible, and user-friendly.

Several tools and frameworks are available to support comprehensive testing efforts across different domains and technologies. For example, popular unit testing frameworks like JUnit, NUnit, and pytest provide developers with a robust set of tools for writing and executing unit tests in Java, .NET, and Python applications, respectively. Similarly, frameworks like Selenium and Cypress are widely used for automated functional testing of web applications, enabling developers to simulate user interactions and validate the application's behavior across different browsers and devices. For performance testing, tools like Apache JMeter, Gatling, and Locust offer powerful capabilities for load testing, stress testing, and benchmarking web applications and APIs. Moreover, security testing tools like OWASP ZAP, Burp Suite, and Nessus help identify and mitigate security vulnerabilities in software systems, including web applications, mobile apps, and network infrastructure.

In summary, comprehensive testing frameworks play a crucial role in ensuring the quality, reliability, and security of software applications by providing a structured approach to testing across different stages of the development lifecycle. By embracing automation, continuous integration, and a diverse set of testing techniques and tools, organizations can achieve faster time-to-market, improved software quality, and enhanced customer satisfaction. Integrating security into system testing is essential for ensuring that software applications are resilient to cyber threats and vulnerabilities throughout their development lifecycle. System testing, which involves testing the entire software system as a whole to verify that it meets specified requirements and functions correctly in its intended environment, provides a critical opportunity to assess the security posture of the application and identify potential weaknesses that could be exploited by attackers. By incorporating security testing activities into the system testing process, organizations can proactively identify and mitigate security risks, safeguard sensitive data, and protect against unauthorized access, data breaches, and other security incidents.

One of the key aspects of integrating security into system testing is the adoption of a comprehensive security testing strategy that encompasses a variety of testing techniques and methodologies. This includes static analysis, dynamic analysis, penetration testing, security scanning, and code review, among others. Static analysis tools, such as static application security testing (SAST) tools, analyze the source code of the application to identify potential security vulnerabilities, such as buffer overflows, injection flaws, and insecure cryptographic algorithms. These tools can be integrated into the software development process to automatically identify security issues early in the development lifecycle, allowing developers to address them before they propagate into production.

Dynamic analysis techniques, such as dynamic application security testing (DAST) and runtime application self-protection (RASP), involve evaluating the application's behavior in a live environment to identify security vulnerabilities and weaknesses. DAST tools simulate real-world attack scenarios by sending malicious input to the application and observing its responses, allowing testers to identify vulnerabilities such as injection flaws, broken authentication, and insecure session management. RASP solutions, on the other hand, monitor the application's runtime behavior and automatically block suspicious activities or malicious inputs, providing an additional layer of protection against security threats.

Penetration testing, also known as ethical hacking, involves simulating real-world cyber attacks to identify vulnerabilities and weaknesses in the application's defenses. Penetration testers, or "white hat" hackers, use a variety of techniques and tools to exploit security vulnerabilities and gain unauthorized access to the application's resources, data, or functionality. By conducting penetration tests, organizations can identify security weaknesses that may not be detected by automated tools or static analysis, allowing them to prioritize remediation efforts and strengthen their security posture.

Security scanning tools, such as vulnerability scanners and web application firewalls (WAFs), automate the process of identifying security vulnerabilities and weaknesses in software applications. Vulnerability scanners scan the application's code, configuration, and dependencies for known security vulnerabilities and misconfigurations, providing organizations with a comprehensive view of their security posture and potential areas of risk. WAFs, on the other hand, monitor and filter HTTP traffic between the application and the user, blocking malicious requests and protecting against common web-based attacks, such as SQL injection, cross-site scripting (XSS), and cross-site request forgery (CSRF).

Code review is another critical aspect of integrating security into system testing, as it involves manually reviewing the application's source code to identify security vulnerabilities and weaknesses that may have been missed by automated testing tools. Code reviews allow developers and security experts to identify insecure coding practices, design flaws, and logic errors that could potentially be exploited by attackers. By incorporating security-focused code review practices, such as threat modeling and security code reviews, organizations can identify and remediate security vulnerabilities early in the development process, reducing the risk of security breaches and data leaks in production.

In addition to adopting a comprehensive security testing strategy, organizations should also ensure that security considerations are integrated into the overall system testing process. This includes defining security requirements and acceptance criteria, conducting security-focused test case design and execution, and documenting security test results and findings. By treating security as an integral part of the system testing process, organizations can effectively identify, prioritize, and mitigate security risks throughout the software development lifecycle, ultimately enhancing the security and resilience of their software applications against evolving cyber threats.

Conclusion

In summary, the "Debugging Playbook" bundle offers a comprehensive guide to mastering the intricacies of system testing, error localization, and vulnerability remediation. Through four meticulously crafted books, readers have been equipped with the fundamental principles, advanced techniques, and expert strategies needed to navigate the complexities of debugging in today's software landscape.

In "Debugging Playbook: System Testing Fundamentals" (Book 1), readers have gained a solid foundation in system testing, learning essential concepts, methodologies, and best practices for ensuring the quality and reliability of software systems. From understanding the fundamentals of system testing to deploying effective testing frameworks, this book has provided readers with the necessary knowledge and skills to excel in the field of software testing.

Building upon this foundation, "Debugging Playbook: Mastering Error Localization Techniques" (Book 2) delves into the art of error localization, offering readers a deep dive into advanced techniques and methodologies for identifying, isolating, and resolving software bugs. Through practical examples, case studies, and hands-on exercises, readers have honed their skills in pinpointing and troubleshooting a wide range of software defects, enabling them to streamline their debugging process and deliver more robust and reliable software solutions.

In "Debugging Playbook: Advanced Strategies for Vulnerability Remediation" (Book 3), readers have explored the intricacies of vulnerability remediation, learning how to identify, prioritize, and mitigate security vulnerabilities in software applications. From understanding common security threats to implementing proactive security measures, this book has empowered readers to strengthen the security posture of their software systems and protect against evolving cyber threats.

Finally, in "Debugging Playbook: Expert Approaches to Comprehensive System Testing and Security" (Book 4), readers have been introduced to expert-level approaches and techniques for comprehensive system testing and security. From incorporating security into the testing process to leveraging advanced debugging tools and methodologies, this book has provided readers with the insights and strategies needed to elevate their debugging skills to the next level and ensure the resilience and reliability of their software applications in today's dynamic and ever-changing technological landscape.

Together, the "Debugging Playbook" bundle serves as an invaluable resource for software developers, testers, and security professionals alike, offering a comprehensive roadmap for mastering the art and science of debugging. Whether you are a seasoned veteran looking to sharpen your skills or a newcomer seeking to learn the ropes, this bundle provides the knowledge, tools, and techniques needed to succeed in the challenging and rewarding field of software debugging.

www.ingramcontent.com/pod-product-compliance
Lightning Source LLC
Chambersburg PA
CBHW070935050326
40689CB00014B/3219